NARRATIVE OF THE LIFE OF
FREDERICK
DOUGLASS
AN AMERICAN SLAVE

NOTES

including
- *Life and Background of the Author*
- *List of Characters*
- *Maps*
- *Summaries & Critical Commentaries*
- *Critical Essays*
    "The Meaning of July Fourth for the Negro"
    The Autobiography as Genre, as Authentic Text
    Slavery as a Mythologized Institution
    Slavery in the United States
    The Fugitive Slave Act
    Slavery in Maryland
    Douglass' Canonical Status and the Heroic Tale
    Douglass' Other Autobiographies
- *Genealogies*
- *Review Questions and Essay Topics*
- *Selected Bibliography*

by
John Chua, M.A.
University of Illinois, Champaign-Urbana

D0957139

Cliffs Notes

INCORPORATED
LINCOLN, NEBRASKA 68501

Editor	Consulting Editor
Gary Carey, M.A.	*James L. Roberts, Ph.D.*
University of Colorado	*Department of English*
	University of Nebraska

ISBN 0-8220-0872-6

2000 Printing

Cliffs Notes, Inc.   Lincoln, Nebraska

CONTENTS

Center Spread: Genealogy

NARRATIVE OF THE LIFE OF
FREDERICK DOUGLASS
AN AMERICAN SLAVE

Notes

LIFE AND BACKGROUND OF THE AUTHOR

Frederick Douglass will forever remain one of the most important figures in America's struggle for civil rights and racial equality. His influence can be seen in the politics and writings of almost all major African-American writers, from Richard Wright to Maya Angelou. Douglass, however, is an inspiration to more than just African Americans. He spoke out against oppression throughout America and abroad, and his struggle for freedom, self-discovery, and identity stands as a testament for all time, for all people. Born into slavery around 1818, he eventually escaped and became a respected American diplomat, a counselor to four presidents, a highly regarded orator, and an influential writer. He accomplished all of these feats without any formal education.

His *Narrative of the Life of Frederick Douglass, an American Slave* is a moving account of the courage of one man's struggle against the injustice of antebellum slavery. Published in 1845, sixteen years before the Civil War began, the *Narrative* describes Douglass' life from early childhood until his escape from slavery in 1838. Douglass uses a matter-of-fact voice, logical analysis, and a dignified tone, but no one can read his account without feeling emotionally sickened by the horrors of slavery. Produced in an era before visual and audio electronic recordings were possible, Douglass' *Narrative* is an important testimony. Had there not been literate slaves who wrote about their sufferings, our knowledge and understanding of this shameful period of America's past might well be different.

Early Life. Douglass was born Frederick Augustus Washington Bailey in Tuckahoe, Maryland, the child of Harriet Bailey, a literate slave. He didn't know who his father was, but, near the beginning of the *Narrative*, Douglass suggests that his white master may have been his father. He recalls meeting his mother only four or five times. She was assigned to work in a field many miles away and was not allowed to stay with her son, seeing him only furtively during rare visits at night. Frederick was initially raised by his grandparents, Betsey and Isaac Bailey, and later by Captain Anthony, who owned two or three farms and about thirty slaves; he was a clerk and superintendent for Colonel Lloyd's plantation. In one of the most poignant episodes at the beginning of the *Narrative*, Douglass recalls being treated like an animal and having to live in the same breeding pens as the plantation's dogs and pigs.

Learning to Read. When he was about eight years old, Frederick was sent to Baltimore to work for Hugh Auld, Captain Anthony's relative by marriage. At first, he was treated with great kindness by Sophia Auld; her husband, Hugh, however, eventually disapproved of Sophia's attempts to teach Frederick how to read and write. Such skills, he reasoned, would make Frederick "unfit . . . to be a slave." But Frederick was determined to have an education, and he convinced the neighborhood children to help him learn. At the shipyard where he worked, he copied the scribbles of other workers to practice writing. He purchased the *Columbian Orator*, as well as the *Baltimore American*. From newspapers, he not only improved his reading ability but discovered for the first time the existence of anti-slavery movements in the North. The activists in these movements were known as abolitionists, and there were different camps within the abolitionist movement. Some of them were led by religious leaders and were closely connected with Northern Protestant churches.

Resistance. Upon Captain Anthony's death in 1833, Frederick was returned to rural Maryland and eventually became the property of Thomas Auld. Considered too "independent" by his new owner, teenage Frederick was placed in the care of Edward Covey, a man who had a reputation as a fierce slave-breaker. Covey beat him mercilessly and without justification. Douglass considered the turning point in his life to be the moment when he resisted Covey's beating. Covey couldn't break his spirit, and, for the first time in Frederick's life, a white man backed down.

Escape. After Covey, Frederick was hired out to William Freeland and attempted an unsuccessful escape with five other slaves. Eventually he was returned to Baltimore, and Hugh Auld rented him out to work in the shipyards. On September 3, 1838, with the help of a freedwoman, Anna Murray (who later became his wife), he escaped to New York City, disguised as a free sailor. In the *Narrative*, Douglass is not forthcoming about his exact escape route. Slavery still existed, and he didn't want to prevent other slaves from escaping in a similar way.

In New York, Douglass soon discovered that living as a refugee and hiding from slave hunters was not easy, so he accepted help from abolitionists who provided shelter and passage to New Bedford, Massachusetts. It was then that he changed his last name to "Douglass" in order to take possession of his own life and fate. On arriving in New Bedford, Frederick and Anna lived with Nathan Johnson, and it was Johnson who suggested that Frederick change his name. "Bailey" was too dangerous and could lead to his capture. Johnson suggested "Douglass" because he admired the heroic Scottish hero of Sir Walter Scott's *Lady of the Lake*.

Freedom. The enterprising Douglass found himself many jobs, including working as a day laborer in a brass foundry, as well as unloading ships. In 1841, Douglass attended an anti-slavery meeting in Nantucket and befriended two well-known abolitionists, John A. Collins and William Lloyd Garrison. Meeting these men proved to be yet another turning point in his life. Collins invited him to be a salaried lecturer, and Douglass agreed to the arrangement for three months. He was such a popular speaker that three months of lectures and tours became four years. In 1845, he decided to put the speeches he gave about his life as a slave into writing. These speeches became the basis for his *Narrative of the Life of Frederick Douglass, an American Slave*.

The work became an instant bestseller in America as well as in Europe, where it was translated into French and German. Despite its critical and popular acclaim, however, it was met with skepticism by pro-slavery Americans, who simply could not believe that such a brilliant account could be produced by a slave with no formal education. Some thought that the text was a clever counterfeit document produced by abolitionists and passed off as Douglass' writing. In fact, Douglass was so frequently confronted by such skeptics in the North that he had to finally demonstrate his oratory skills in order to prove his intellectual capacity.

Because of the fame created by his *Narrative*, Douglass risked capture by slave hunters in the North, so he sailed for England. For two years, he lectured on the evils of slavery. He found the British sympathetic to the abolitionists' cause but ignorant of the horrific conditions of slavery in America. Through some British friends, Douglass discovered that Thomas Auld was willing to sell Douglass' freedom for $711.16, and two of his English friends paid the price and bought his freedom. In 1847, Douglass returned to America as a free man.

The Years Preceding and During the Civil War. Not long afterward, Douglass began to break with his former abolitionist protectors. Although still a fervent anti-slavery advocate, he didn't want to be the mouthpiece of white abolitionists who sometimes told him to "dumb down" his speeches in order to sound more like an authentic slave. He felt excluded from major political decisions made by those who ran the abolitionist societies. In addition, the Garrisonian wing of the abolitionist movement was simply not aggressive enough for Douglass.

In 1855, Douglass updated his autobiography and called it *My Bondage and My Freedom*. In it, he presented more of his views and also included some of his ideas about the anti-slavery crusade. Douglass believed that physical resistance and slave uprisings should remain viable options. Accordingly, he was a supporter of John Brown, who raided the arsenal at Harper's Ferry in 1859 as part of a plan to incite a general slave uprising in the South. Brown and his associates were defeated by U.S. troops, led by Colonel Robert E. Lee (who later became the commanding general of the Confederate forces). Brown and the surviving conspirators were executed in Virginia after a sham trial. While Douglass was not directly involved in John Brown's raid, he nevertheless fled to Canada and, soon afterward, to England in November 1859.

Six months later, Douglass learned of the death of his daughter and returned to America, where he worked for the election campaign of Abraham Lincoln in 1860, calling Lincoln a man "destined to do greater service to his country and to mankind than any man who [has] gone before him in the presidential office."

When the Civil War erupted, Douglass worked hard to persuade the Union to accept blacks in the military. Governor Andrew of Massachusetts was allowed by President Lincoln to organize two black regiments, the famed 54th and 55th. (Their heroism is depicted in the movie *Glory*.) Two of Douglass' sons, Charles and Lewis, joined the black regiments, knowing full well that captured black Union soldiers were not treated well by Southerners; they were either shot or sold into slavery. Douglass pressured Lincoln to obtain assurance from Jefferson Davis of the Confederacy that this practice would be reversed, but Lincoln never received it. In October 1864, Douglass met with other blacks at a convention in Syracuse, New York, to discuss the future of African Americans in a post-Civil War America. Douglass pushed for universal suffrage for black Americans, but faced opposition from ambivalent racist whites and even from the Garrisonian wing of the abolitionist movement.

After the North defeated Southern forces in Atlanta, Georgia, and in Richmond, Virginia, Lincoln won at the polls, and on April 9, 1865, General Lee of the Confederate Army surrendered to General Grant, the Union commander. Although sporadic fighting continued, the Civil War was effectively over.

On April 14, 1865, Lincoln was assassinated by John Wilkes Booth, and the assassination ironically gave a boost to the civil rights movement. The ideals of the martyred president became a rallying force for pro-Union Americans. In the heady days of victory over the South, Congress passed the Thirteenth and Fourteenth Amendments. For the first time, citizenship was defined by the Constitution and was extended to *all* people born within the United States—including blacks—but excluding Native Americans.

The Post-War Years. Following the Civil War, Douglass worked to elect Republican party candidates and also worked for black suffrage. He returned to the lecture circuit in 1874 after his newspaper, *The New National Era,* and a bank for freed slaves failed. The bank, of which Douglass had been appointed president three months earlier, had a deficit of $200,000. The trustees thought Douglass' appointment would bring prestige and inspire confidence in black depositors, but that didn't happen. (Douglass was unaware of the bank's perilous financial situation when he accepted the job.)

Shortly after the bank failed, he began lecturing again to make ends meet. His oratory skills gained him a new reputation, and he was in demand again, earning as much as $100 to $200 per lecture, considerable sums in those days.

Douglass remained close to many Republican politicians, including President Grant, who offered him a short-term commission in January 1871 to investigate whether the United States should annex the Caribbean country of Santo Domingo. Douglass believed in the American dream of personal success. He believed that the people of Santo Domingo could benefit from American institutions, values, capitalism, and know-how, and he supported American annexation. Some scholars, particularly those belonging to the School of New Historicism, believe that this philosophy, on a national level, became an American ideology of political, economical, and geographical expansion, an expansionist ideology referred to in the nineteenth century as the doctrine of **Manifest Destiny.** Ultimately, Grant's ambition to annex Santo Domingo was opposed by his political enemies and his plan never took effect. After returning from the Caribbean, Douglass labored for Grant's reelection. He expected to be appointed to an office, but no appointment was forthcoming. He was, however, appointed U.S. Marshal of the District of Columbia in 1877 by Rutherford B. Hayes, and in 1878, he was financially secure enough to buy a fifteen-acre estate and a large house in Washington, D.C. In 1881, he updated his autobiography again, calling it *The Life and Times of Frederick Douglass.*

In August 1882, Douglass' wife, Anna, died after forty-four years of marriage. Douglass was consoled by a number of their female friends, including many white women in the suffrage and abolitionist movements. The suffragettes were activists who fought for women's rights, including the right for women to vote, and, as civil rights activists, they shared many of the goals of the anti-slavery movement. Susan B. Anthony, possibly the most famous of the nineteenth-century suffragettes, was a good friend of Douglass' and would give his funeral oration.

Douglass enjoyed flaunting his friendships with white women and explained that such relationships confronted racism head-on.

Historians now believe that Douglass had an affair for over twenty years, from 1856 to 1881, with Ottilie Assing, a German journalist and political radical. But Assing was more than a lover;

she was Douglass' intellectual partner. The two spent much time together, reading everything from Shakespeare to Marx. Assing's letters, discovered in Poland in the late 1980s, have helped historians understand their sexual relationship. As someone who was overtly Christian, as well as a leader in the African-American community, Douglass was naturally very secretive about his affairs. None of his three autobiographies reveal much about his wife or his liaisons with other women. A year and a half after his wife died, he married Helen Pitts, his white secretary, who worked for the Recorder of Deeds. Assing committed suicide soon afterward, but left a trust fund for Douglass. Many blacks and whites were shocked by his second marriage, but Douglass argued that black and white sexual relations had always existed in the United States; he had merely legitimized it with marriage.

In 1888, Douglass worked for Benjamin Harrison's campaign for the presidency. Upon becoming president, Harrison rewarded Douglass with the post of Ambassador to Haiti. Returning from Haiti, Douglass spent his remaining years writing and lecturing about the lynching of blacks, their deprivation of civil rights in the South, and the growing use of Jim Crow laws. These laws prevented blacks from voting by requiring a literacy test, the payment of property taxes, and other unconstitutional measures. They also prevented blacks from participating in government and, in general, stripped them of their constitutional rights.

Douglass died of heart failure on February 20, 1895, at the age of approximately seventy-seven. He had lived a long life by nineteenth-century standards—particularly, for a black man. More significantly, however, he had lived an extraordinary life, overcoming all odds to become one of the greatest figures in American history.

LIST OF CHARACTERS

William Lloyd Garrison

A leading abolitionist in the North, and Douglass' patron. Garrison and his followers advocated the abolition of slavery on moral grounds but did not support armed resistance.

Wendell Phillips

Another leading figure in the abolitionist movement. After the Civil War, Phillips supported Douglass' position regarding the enfranchisement of freed slaves. The Phillips-Douglass alliance was in direct opposition to Garrison and his supporters, who advocated a slower pace of reform.

Harriet Bailey

Douglass' mother; little is known about her. Years after her death, Douglass learned that she was a literate slave. He was never able to determine, though, how a field hand had the opportunity to learn to read.

Captain Anthony

Douglass' first master and possibly his father. Captain Anthony was Colonel Lloyd's clerk and superintendent. His children were Andrew, Richard, and Lucretia.

Colonel Lloyd

Lloyd was reportedly the richest slave holder in Talbot County, Maryland. The Lloyd family had been in Maryland for over two hundred years, and many of its members were politicians and prominent people in Maryland society. Colonel Lloyd behaved almost like a feudal lord of the region.

Mr. Severe

A cruel and profane overseer; his early death was considered an act of divine providence by the slaves.

Mr. Gore

Another exceptionally cruel overseer; he had no qualms about executing a slave who disobeyed him.

Mrs. Lucretia Auld

Daughter of Captain Anthony. In *The Life and Times of Frederick Douglass*, Douglass describes Lucretia as a kind woman who protected him from being beaten by Aunt Katy, another slave. In his old age, Douglass became a good friend of Lucretia's daughter, Amanda Auld. Lucretia had died when Amanda was still a child.

Thomas Auld

Upon the death of his wife, Thomas took control of all of her property, including Douglass. Douglass recalls him as a hypocritical and cruel master. Thomas loaned Douglass to his brother Hugh Auld in Baltimore, as well as to Covey, a slave-breaker. On his death bed, Thomas asked to see Douglass.

Hugh Auld

A ship-builder in Baltimore. Douglass portrays him as a greedy slave master who exploited Douglass as a day worker. Hugh prohibited Douglass from learning to read because he felt a knowledgeable slave was a dangerous one.

Sophia Auld

The wife of Hugh Auld. At first, she was exceedingly kind to Douglass, but owning slaves corrupted her and eventually led her to treat him as mere property.

Edward Covey

Thomas Auld loaned Douglass to Covey, a poor farmer famous in Talbot County as an unparalleled breaker of slaves. Covey's duty was to crush Douglass' rebellious spirit. In return, Covey acquired free use of Douglass for a year. Covey was sneaky and cruel, nick-named "the snake" by his slaves. Eventually Douglass successfully confronted Covey and was never whipped again.

Sandy Jenkins

A superstitious slave who showed Douglass how to protect himself from Covey with a magical root. Following Jenkins' instruction, Douglass found himself able to confront Covey. This is a puzzling episode because Douglass does not really explain whether he believed the magical root worked or whether it simply gave him a psychological boost.

Douglass was born around 1818 to a slave woman who lived in the Tidewater area of Maryland. He never knew his father, but he suspected that his master, Captain Anthony, had probably fathered him. Until he was seven or eight, he lived on Colonel Lloyd's plantation. At that time, he was sent to Baltimore to live with relatives of Captain Anthony, Hugh and Sophia Auld, where he spent the next seven years, learning to read and write in secret. Upon the deaths of both of Captain Anthony's children, because Douglass was considered "property" belonging to them, he was passed on to another relative, Thomas Auld, who lived in St. Michaels, Talbot County, Maryland.

Douglass soon gained a reputation as a troublemaker and was eventually sent to live once again with Thomas' brother, Hugh. On Chesapeake Bay, Douglass was able to watch ships sailing toward the Northern states. He vowed to himself that someday he would be free.

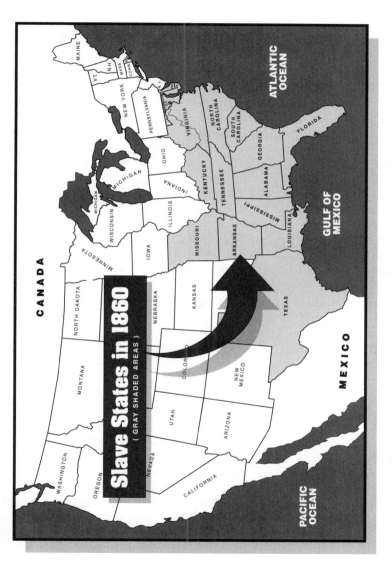

Slave States in 1860
(GRAY SHADED AREAS)

The freeing of slaves in the North and the opening up of new territories in the West made fugitive slaves a national issue. The Fugitive Slave Act stipulated that slave owners or their agents could arrest and return escaped slaves from any territory or state. Anyone hindering the arrest or providing haven to fugitive slaves was also liable for arrest.

SUMMARIES & CRITICAL COMMENTARIES

GARRISON'S PREFACE AND LETTER TO DOUGLASS

Certain editions of the *Narrative* begin with a preface by William Lloyd Garrison and a letter to Douglass from Wendell Phillips. Garrison, a well-known abolitionist, begins his preface by telling us he met Douglass at an abolitionist convention and that the former slave's speech so impressed the audience that Garrison felt he "never hated slavery so intensely as at that moment." He adds that Patrick Henry, the American patriot and revolutionary famous for his "Give me liberty or give me death" speech, "never made a speech more eloquent in the cause of liberty, than the one we had just listened to [at that convention] from the lips of that hunted fugitive."

Garrison emphasizes that institutionalized oppression can adversely affect anyone—not just slaves. He explains that a white person can be reduced to the intellectual level of an animal—if oppressed to excess—and he offers an anecdote about a white American sailor who, after having been captured and kept as a slave for three years in Africa, "lost all reasoning power." Slavery surely cripples the intellect, he reasons, and thus, the abolitionist movement is indeed fortunate to include Douglass, someone who has lived through the brutality of slavery but still retains the ability for coherent advocacy.

Garrison testifies that Douglass himself wrote his *Narrative:* "I am confident that it is essentially true in all its statements; that nothing has been set down in malice, nothing exaggerated, nothing drawn from the imagination." Garrison vouches that any reader unaffected by Douglass' story must indeed have a heart of stone. He adds that Douglass' experiences as a slave are not unique and that there are certainly slaves in Georgia, Alabama, and Louisiana who are even more badly treated than slaves in Maryland.

There are those, Garrison warns, who "are stubbornly incredulous whenever they read or listen to any recital of the cruelties which are inflicted on [slaves]." These people will try "to discredit the shocking tales of slaveholding cruelty which are recorded in this truthful Narrative." Garrison, however, is confident that these skeptics will not be able to find falsehoods in the stories Douglass tells.

He ends his preface by mentioning two matters which Douglass later stresses in the *Narrative*: (1) slaves have no legal recourse; they cannot appeal to any legal authority for the cruelties inflicted upon them by their masters; (2) those people who favor slavery are not on the side of God and Christianity.

Commentary

The entire preface can be considered a classic example of a rhetorical essay, complete with an introduction to the subject (Douglass-as-slave), arguments against slavery (on moral, judicial, scientific, and religious grounds), and a call to arms. William Lloyd Garrison (1805–1879) was a journalist, social reformer, and a leading figure in the abolitionist movement, and his preface can be seen as an excellent **rhetorical strategy** for the entire work because it is an endorsement of Douglass' story, as well as for the veracity of the *Narrative*. There were many skeptics from both the North and South who did not believe that an escaped, uneducated slave could have written such a narrative, nor did they believe the detailed atrocities that were said to exist in the slave states.

Garrison's reference to Patrick Henry is an attempt to raise Douglass to the level of a great American patriot—that is, the freedoms that Douglass is fighting for are the same freedoms that the early American revolutionaries wanted for themselves. Garrison argues that slaves are human beings who must be given the same rights afforded to other Americans. Garrison brings up an example of an enslaved white American, arguing that slavery reduces the reasoning powers of *all* humans—regardless of race. He does this as a **pre-emptive argument** against those who would propose that Africans are intellectually inferior (and that, accordingly, slaveholders are actually "taking care" of them as they would their livestock). Garrison argues that slaves are just like other human beings and thus they must be given the same legal protection as whites have. The inequality of blacks under the law makes the entire slave system unjustifiable. Garrison proclaims that if America truly believes in democracy, justice, and equality, then slavery cannot exist within this system. On a final note, Garrison makes a powerful call to action for all Christians to resist the slave system; he concludes that those who are truly on the side of God must also be against slavery.

18

(Here and in the following chapters, difficult allusions, words, and phrases are explained.)

- **Patrick Henry** (1736–1799) an American revolutionary, famous for his "Give me liberty or give me death" stance.
- **Charles Renox Remond** (1810–1873) another black orator who toured with Douglass, giving anti-slavery speeches.
- **Alexandrian Library** the greatest library in the classical world, located in northern Egypt, on the Mediterranean Sea.
- **flagellation** flogging.

LETTER FROM WENDELL PHILLIPS, ESQ.

A private letter from Phillips, addressing Douglass as "My Dear Friend," is sometimes included as an introduction to certain editions of the *Narrative*. Phillips begins his letter by referring to the old fable of "The Man and the Lion," in which the lion states that he would no longer be misrepresented if he—and *not the man*—could tell his side of the story. Such is the condition of the slave, whose true story is not usually told; instead, the slave masters have always spoken on behalf of the slave.

Phillips refers to the West Indian "experiment" of 1838, when Britain finally abolished the slave trade and granted freedom to blacks throughout the British colonies. Sadly, the success of this emancipation brought few converts to the abolition movement. Too many people have continued to be more concerned about the price of sugar than they are about the victims of slavery.

Phillips urges Douglass to fairly compare how his race is treated in the North and in the South and tell readers about the differences. He wants to thank Douglass for fully revealing the horrors of slavery. Douglass, he says, has shown immense courage. It is exceedingly dangerous to expose one's identity through the media, for slave hunters will be eager to track down just such a fugitive. Phillips admits that if he were Douglass he would not have the courage to publish this manuscript; he would throw it in the fire in order to avoid publicity. Phillips hopes for the day when the North need no longer simply hide fugitives but openly welcome them. New England, which was a place of refuge for the Pilgrims, should now be an open asylum for all oppressed peoples.

Commentary

Wendell Phillips was another leading abolitionist of the time, and his letter serves as a kind of "book review." Phillips begins by recognizing that history is told by people who hold power. Marginalized people are misrepresented or misunderstood because they have no voice. Phillips' argument is, in fact, surprisingly similar to that made by political activists in the U.S. today, who demand that marginalized people—people of color, women, racial minorities, gays and lesbians—be represented.

Phillips refers to the anti-slavery movement in Britain which ended slavery in British colonies in the Caribbean (West Indies). The "experiment" apparently had no horrendous or negative effect on British society or on its economy. Furthermore, Phillips urges abolitionists to look beyond simple moral arguments. For example, he cites abolitionists whose only argument is that it is not right for Southerners to justify slavery on *economic* grounds. (Some pro-slavery advocates warned that eliminating slavery in the Caribbean would lead to an increase in the price of sugar.) There are many other arguments one can make against slavery, Phillips says, presenting slavery as an issue that is absolutely antithetical to the very foundations of a free America. Plymouth Rock once offered refuge to the oppressed; it should do so again.

Phillips' comments about fugitive slaves being hunted refers to the existence of slave hunters, whose sole livelihood was capturing fugitives in the North for a bounty. Slave hunters were later legitimized under the **Fugitive Slave Act**. As part of the Great Compromise of 1850, Congress passed a bill forbidding new slave states but allowing fugitive slaves to be captured and returned to their owners. The measure preserved the Union for a few more years.

Phillips understands that there is racism in the North, that the black person there enjoys only partial rights ("a twilight of rights"), but this situation, he feels, is better than the "noon of night" (midnight), under which slaves labor in the South.

- **a halter about their neck**   a rope around their neck, or in danger of death.

- **desolate**   a deserted place.

- **MS**   the abbreviation for manuscript.

CHAPTER I

Douglass begins his *Narrative* by explaining that he is like many other slaves who don't know when they were born and, sometimes, even who their parents are. From hearsay, he estimates that he was born around 1817 and that his father was probably his first white master, Captain Anthony. His mother, Harriet Bailey, was a field hand who wasn't allowed to see him very often; she died when Douglass was seven years old. Children of mixed race parentage are always classified as slaves, Douglass says, and this class of mulattos is increasing rapidly. Douglass implies that these mulatto slaves are, for the most part, the result of white masters raping black slaves. He tells about the brutality of his master's overseer, Mr. Plummer, as well as the story of Aunt Hester, who was brutally whipped by Captain Anthony because she fancied another slave. Captain Anthony apparently wanted her for himself exclusively.

Commentary

From the very beginning of his *Narrative*, Douglass shocks and horrifies his readers. Not only does he vividly detail the physical cruelties inflicted on slaves, but he also presents a frank discussion about sex between white male owners and female slaves.

Like other autobiographers of his time, Douglass chooses to begin his story by telling when and where he was born. However, this is impossible, he says, because slave owners keep slaves ignorant about their age and parentage in order to strip them of their identities. (Douglass is also implying that this ploy is also a refusal by white owners to acknowledge their carnal natures.) Slaves are thus reduced to the level of animals: "Slaves know as little of their ages as horses know of theirs." The **tone** of this passage is simple and factual, presented with little emotion, yet the reader cannot help feeling outraged by it. The separation of mother and child is another way slave owners control their slaves, preventing slave children from developing familial bonds, loyalty to another slave, and a knowledge of heritage and identity.

Douglass' underlying tone is bitter, especially about his white father creating him and then abandoning him to slavery. He immediately tackles an uncomfortable topic for the readers of his and our times—the rape of black women by white men with power. According to Douglass, the children of white masters and female slaves generally receive the worst treatment of all, and the master is frequently compelled to sell his mulatto children "out of deference to the feelings of his white wife." For the wife, her husband's mulatto children are living reminders of his infidelity.

With a single bold stroke, Douglass **deconstructs** one of the myths of slavery. In the nineteenth century, Southerners believed that God cursed Ham, the son of Noah, by turning his skin black and his descendants into slaves. For Southerners, therefore, the descendants of Ham were predestined by the scriptures to be slaves. However, Douglass asks, if only blacks are "scripturally enslaved," why should mixed-race children be also destined for slavery? Douglass wonders if it's possible that this class of mulatto slaves might someday become so large that their population will exceed that of the whites. Beneath his bitterness is a belief that time is on his side; the natural laws of population expansion will allow his people to prevail.

Douglass concludes this chapter by devoting a long section to childhood memories, to the first time he witnessed a slave being beaten. Later, the extended description of the cruelty inflicted on Aunt Hester **foreshadows** the kind of brutality to come: "I expected it would be my turn next." Douglass has come to realize that sexuality and power are inseparable. He strongly implies that Captain Anthony's beating of Hester is the result of his jealousy, for Hester had taken an interest in a fellow slave.

- **odiousness**   contemptible, detestable.

- **overseer**   one who manages slaves and keeps them well disciplined and productive.

CHAPTER II

Douglass describes his master's family and their relationship with Colonel Lloyd, who was sort of a "grand master" of the area. Douglass explains that if slaves broke plantation rules, tried to run away, or became generally "unmanageable," they were whipped and shipped to Baltimore to be sold to slave traders as a "warning to the [other] slaves." He discusses the meager food and clothing allowance given to slaves: "Children from seven to ten years old, of both sexes, almost naked, might be seen all seasons of the year." Slaves had no beds and only some were given blankets. They had to work long hours in the fields and were deprived of sleep. The master's latest overseer, with the fitting name of Mr. Severe, was "armed with a large hickory stick and heavy cowskin" and took "fiendish pleasure in manifesting barbarity." Severe's early death was considered a sign of a "merciful providence" by the slaves, but he was soon replaced by Hopkins, a less profane man, but no less cruel than Severe.

The home plantation of Colonel Lloyd was called the Great House Farm, and it was a privilege for a slave in the outlying areas of the plantation to be asked to run errands there. Many of the songs that slaves sang at that plantation mention the Great House Farm; Douglass didn't understand the implications of the lyrics of the songs while he was enslaved, but as a free man in the North, he has heard whites commenting that the singing of slaves is "evidence of their contentment and happiness." He refutes this myth, stating that slaves sing in order to relieve their sorrow, much like tears relieve an aching heart.

Commentary

Besides the master-slave division, Douglass points out that within the slave-owning class, there is also a hierarchy. Douglass' master, Captain Anthony, worked as a clerk and superintendent for Colonel Lloyd, who would have been considered virtually a feudal lord of the region. Captain Anthony was not a rich slaveholder, but he had slaves and hired hands working for him.

As bad as conditions were for slaves in that part of Maryland, conditions were far worse on Deep South plantations. Although Douglass does not explicitly mention or state details, conditions in Georgian plantations, for example, were much worse for slaves than they were in Maryland.

Douglass' mention of other slaves' belief that divine retribution was responsible for the agonizing death of Mr. Severe is somewhat curious because despite Douglass' religiosity, he does not say whether or not he believes in this "merciful retribution."

While Douglass does not use the term **false consciousness** (a Marxist concept which proposes that workers are fooled into believing in and contributing to a system benefitting only those in power), he is essentially debunking this false consciousness of slaves who believed that being chosen to serve Colonel Lloyd was a great honor.

Slaves were led to believe in a false system of values, where certain tasks were considered more prestigious than others; in fact, however, all tasks performed by slaves should be considered unacceptable.

Douglass also debunks the ignorance of Northern whites who believe that the sound of slaves singing on plantations is a sign of their happiness. If Douglass were alive today, he would perhaps find it **ironic** that today's mainstream blues and pop music have their origins in the grieving music of a disenfranchised people.

- **blasphemy**   profane, a sacrilege.

- **jargon**   idioms; words used within a subculture.

CHAPTER III

When Douglass went to live at Colonel Lloyd's plantation, he was awed by the splendor he saw. Douglass heard that Lloyd owned approximately a thousand slaves, and he believes that this estimate is probably accurate. Lloyd was especially renowned for his beautiful garden, which people traveled many miles to view. Unfortunately, the garden had an abundance of tempting fruits which were off-limits to the hungry slaves, who were whipped if they were caught stealing fruit. The crafty colonel spread tar around the garden to catch thieves, and the mere evidence of tar on a slave was sufficient grounds for a lashing. The colonel also had a stable of splendid horses, which he clearly loved more than his slaves. The slaves who took care of the horses were frequently whipped for not performing their duties to the colonel's precise demands.

Because Colonel Lloyd owned so many slaves, some of them never met him. Not surprisingly, one day while riding around the large plantation, he met a slave and asked him who his master was and how his master treated him. When he heard negative comments, he would note who the slave was and arranged to have that slave sold to a Georgian slave trader.

Douglass explains that owners often send in colored spies among their own slaves to determine their views about their living and working conditions. For this reason, many slaves, when asked by other slaves about their living conditions, simply lie and present a pleasing picture of slavery. Strangely enough, slaves often seem to feel particularly proud of their affiliation with their owner when confronting slaves owned by a different owner, and fistfights are often the result of heated discussions among slaves, regarding whose owner is better, stronger, or richer.

Commentary

Douglass is implicit in his criticism that the splendor of Colonel Lloyd's estate was made possible only by the toil of slaves. Ironically, in a cruel gesture, slaves were never allowed to enjoy the fruits of their labor. In fact, slaves were constantly kept hungry.

In this and other chapters, Douglass presents a vast panorama of slaves under constant surveillance. Not only do slave owners lay traps to catch slaves breaking rules, he says, but they want to eliminate all dissenting slaves. And they accomplish this end by various means, including spying and **entrapment**. The constant surveillance by owners is one of many ways slaves are intimidated and brainwashed into believing that their lot is better than it really is. In effect, slaves are unconscious of their reality. This fact is illustrated by the example of slaves fighting among themselves to determine whose owner is better. Douglass condemns this false consciousness which destroys **solidarity** among slaves. Perversely, loyalty has become a matter of pledging allegiance to one's *owner* and not to one's *brother*.

Douglass is repeatedly critical of the slave owners' value system. Not only do owners treat slaves like animals, but they usually value animals more than their slaves. Lloyd certainly mistreated his slaves but never his horses; Douglass says that such a system which prizes animals over humans is heinous. Lloyd likewise meted out punishment in an arbitrary manner; because the horse handlers (the two Barneys) could never satisfy him, Lloyd's justice exemplified the capricious system of slavery.

- **ascertain**   to make certain.

- **imbibe**   to absorb; to take part in.

- **Jacob Jepson**   a rich slave owner, a neighbor of Colonel Lloyd's.

CHAPTER IV

Hopkins was eventually replaced by Gore, an ambitious over-seer who was exceptionally cruel. Douglass remembers an episode when Gore whipped a slave named Demby so badly that Demby ran into a deep, flowing creek to soothe his shoulders. Gore warned that he would shoot if Demby didn't come out of the creek. Gore counted to three, and Demby still failed to emerge from the creek. Without further warning, Gore cocked his musket and killed Demby. Gore later explained to Lloyd that the killing served as an example to other slaves: disobey—and die. Douglass elaborates that killing a slave is not considered a crime by the courts nor by the community in Maryland. He provides two more examples of owners who murdered their slaves but escaped punishment from the courts and censure from the community.

Commentary

Slave owners and their overseers are the law. This chapter makes it clear that slaves live in continual terror and in an extrajudicial system. Douglass makes an argument here against the existence of two different legal and moral systems, one for whites and another for slaves. Again, Douglass illustrates that slave owners rule by example; the horrible punishment exacted on Demby was meant to be an example to others. Slaves are scared into subservience. The control of slaves requires complete physical, as well as mental, submission.

Being an overseer is a career choice, and to be a good one requires certain qualifications. Gore certainly met the standards of being a good overseer. He was ambitious enough to realize that he had to be exceedingly cruel and cold—and his work was soon appreciated by whites, and his fame grew.

From Chapter I to Chapter IV, we have been presented with increasingly atrocious horrors of slavery—and just as we feel that things could not be worse, we are further horrified. Yet Douglass' role up to this point is mainly as a narrator/observer; his detachment is an excellent rhetorical strategy. He wants, first of all, to present examples of evidence in order to fully develop his case. By this point in his testimony, his evidence has certainly swayed most readers.

- **servile** subservient, submissive.

- **arraigned before a court** charged with an offense in court.

CHAPTER V

Douglass further describes the conditions of slave children on Colonel Lloyd's plantation, telling us that his own experience was typical of slave children. Although he was seldom whipped, he was constantly hungry and cold. Even in the dead of winter, he was given nothing but a long shirt to wear, and, at night, he would steal a bag, crawl into it headfirst, and sleep. His exposed feet developed deep cracks from the frost. Children were fed cornmeal mush from a trough on the ground, and they ate from it, like the pigs did.

When he was about seven or eight years old, he was given to Captain Anthony's son-in-law's brother, Hugh Auld, who lived in Baltimore. Douglass was instructed to clean himself before going to Baltimore, and he took great pride and joy in washing himself. He looks upon this event as a turning point in his life and claims that it was the hand of Providence which offered him this opportunity. In Baltimore, Mr. and Mrs. Auld and their child, Thomas, received him kindly. His duty was to take care of young Thomas.

Commentary

Once again, Douglass illustrates how slaves were treated like animals. Because he never really knew his mother (who was already dead, at this point) nor felt connected with his grandmother, who lived far from him on the plantation, he felt he wasn't leaving anything of value behind when he left for Baltimore. Douglass again indicts the practice of breaking up slave families.

Baltimore was a revelation for Douglass. For the first time in his life, he encountered "a white face [Mrs. Auld] beaming with the most kindly emotions." He realized that he no longer need be always afraid of all whites, that there were some whites who would be kind to him. Douglass considers the move to Baltimore a turning point in his life, one which he attributes to divine providence; we should not overlook the fact that Douglass' religion frames the entire *Narrative*. As we shall see later, the *Narrative* presents a battle of two religions—between Douglass' religion and the Christianity of slaveholders. Douglass shows us that the latter is characterized largely by hypocrisy.

- **manifestation**   a show, or demonstration.

- **aft**   toward the back of a boat.

- **bow**   the forward end of a boat.

- **sloop**   a single masted sailing boat.

CHAPTER VI

Mrs. Sophia Auld was unlike any white person Douglass had met before because she had "the kindest heart and finest feelings." She had never owned a slave, and, prior to her marriage, she was an industrious weaver. But her personality soon changed. At first, Mrs. Auld taught Douglass how to read, but Mr. Auld admonished her and explained, "Learning would spoil the best nigger in the world . . . if you teach that nigger . . . how to read, there would be no keeping him. It would forever unfit him to be a slave."

Slaves in the cities were generally treated better than those on plantations. Douglass was better fed and clothed in Baltimore than he had ever been. There were also community standards regarding how slaves should be treated. "Few are willing to incur the odium attaching the reputation of being a cruel master. . . . Every city slaveholder is anxious to have it known of him, that he feeds his slaves well." Douglass, however, ends this chapter with one exception— Mary, a slave in the neighborhood, is treated brutally by her master.

Commentary

In this and the next chapter, Douglass explores how slavery is detrimental to whites. The *Narrative*, after all, is an **advocacy statement**. Douglass wants to convince his white readers in the North and South that slavery is bad on moral, legal, religious, and economic grounds. Here, Douglass shows us how slavery corrupts the morality of whites: initially, Mrs. Sophia Auld was a kind and industrious person, who treated Douglass like a genuine human being because prior to meeting Douglass, she had never owned a slave. In the beginning, Sophia Auld did not understand that teaching

Douglass to read and write would free his mind, a first step toward physical freedom. But after her husband explained to her that freeing Douglass' mind could lead her to losing her property (that is, Douglass himself), she changed her attitude.

Douglass ends this chapter by presenting the horrifying story of Mary, a neighboring slave. He does this because he wants to show that even though slavery in the cities is comparatively better, it is still unacceptable. His point is that wherever there is slavery, there will be mistreated slaves.

- **blighting**   a scourge, devastation.

- **vestige**   a remnant; a trace of.

- **offal**   parts of an animal killed for food, which are thrown away.

- **gip**   a swindler or cheater.

- **ell**   about 45 inches; a British unit of measurement.

CHAPTER VII

Douglass spent about seven years in Master Hugh's house, and, in secret, he learned to read and write during that time, despite the fact that the once-kindly Mrs. Auld soon internalized the evils of being a slave owner. She accepted the advice of her husband and became a strident advocate of keeping slaves illiterate, for she feared losing Douglass if he gained an education. However, Douglass developed schemes to learn how to read; he tricked neighborhood kids into teaching him by giving bread to poor white boys in exchange for lessons, and he practiced writing using little Thomas' books.

Ironically, Douglass' ability to read soon made him unhappy, for it opened up a whole new—and wretched—world for him. From newspapers, he realized the enormity of a people enslaved by powerful white masters. However, newspapers also furnished him information about the abolitionist movements in the North, and he learned about the Irish dramatist and politician Richard Brinsley Sheridan and his struggles for Catholic emancipation and human rights. His spirits began to lift after meeting some sympathetic Irish workers in a shipyard, who advised him to escape to the North. He was only twelve years old, but he resolved that day to eventually run away.

Commentary

Until his arrival in Baltimore, Douglass had been a victim of circumstances; decisions affecting him were made for him. Now, for the first time, he begins to make decisions independent of the people around him. His first major decision is deciding that he wants to learn. His resolve is further strengthened when Hugh Auld tries to prevent him from gaining an education. At that moment, he realizes that the ability of powerful whites to control slaves comes not so much from physical control as it does from **mental domination**. As long as whites can keep slaves ignorant, they can control them. Hugh's diatribe against educating slaves ironically becomes a significant revelation to Douglass: "I now understood . . . the white man's power to enslave the black man . . . I was gladdened by the invaluable instruction which, by the merest accident, I had gained from my master." Douglass was determined to learn to read—at all costs.

Evidential standards for the treatment of slaves in cities were somewhat better than those in the countryside. In the countryside, Lloyd had few white neighbors, so mistreatment was unlikely to be censured by others. In the cities, larger populations subjected slave owners to more public scrutiny. Neighbors thus had a moderating effect on the conduct of slaveholders in the city.

- **chattel**   belongings; property; slaves.

- **divest her of this heavenly quality**   take away the goodness in her.

- *Columbian Orator*   a collection of classic speeches, dialogues, and plays edited by Caleb Bingham and published in 1797. Douglass patterned his own lectures after these classic speeches.

- **Richard Brinsley Sheridan** (1751–1816)   an Irish playwright who argued for Irish emancipation from English rule.

- **larboard**   the left-hand side of a ship, facing forward.

- **starboard**   the right-hand side of a ship, facing forward.

CHAPTER VIII

In a digression, Douglass tells us that about five years after he had been living in Baltimore, his old master, Captain Anthony, died and Douglass was sent back to the plantation for a valuation so that all of the captain's property could be appraised and divided up among his relatives. "Men and women, old and young, married and single, were ranked with horses, sheep, and swine" for the purpose of this evaluation. He was indeed nervous about his future, for it was possible that he would be sold to a crueler master or to a Georgia trader. Anthony had two children, Andrew and Lucretia (a third child had died earlier), and Douglass was awarded to Lucretia, which meant that he would be returned to her relatives (by marriage), the Aulds in Baltimore. This turn of events was fortunate for Douglass because during his short visit, Andrew demonstrated his cruelty by crushing the head of Douglass' brother.

Soon after Douglass' return to Baltimore, both Lucretia and Andrew died, and all of the slaves were once again slated to be sold or given away. Douglass was particularly angry about how his grandmother, after years of service to Anthony, was left to die in an isolated hut in the woods. Lucretia's surviving husband, Master Thomas, now owned Douglass. A misunderstanding arose between Thomas and his brother Hugh Auld, and, as a spiteful gesture, Thomas took Douglass away from Hugh. Douglass was not entirely unhappy to leave Baltimore, for alcohol had changed Hugh's character, just as slavery had corrupted Sophia's.

Commentary

The death of Captain Anthony presented a perilous and frightening time for Douglass. When owners of property died, got married, or changed their familial ties, their property often changed hands. Slaves were particularly afraid of being sold to Georgia traders or to other plantations where conditions were reportedly much worse.

Appraisers valued the slaves much the same way they assessed animals. Douglass' description of the evaluation process may well make us feel uncomfortable. Douglass adds: "At this moment, I saw more clearly than ever the brutalizing effects of slavery upon both slave and slaveholder."

Master Andrew's brutalizing of Douglass' brother is another particularly vivid episode. The fact that it may be one half-brother brutalizing another is an underlying theme. Although Douglass does not mention it, his brother and Andrew could easily have been related since in the beginning of the *Narrative*, he himself speculates that Captain Anthony could have been his father.

Douglass again criticizes the use of female slaves to populate a plantation. He refers to the episode of his abandoned grandmother with great pain; after having served Captain Anthony for many decades, "peopling his plantation with slaves" ("the source of all his wealth"), she is abandoned. The raping of slaves for profit is an implicit sub-text here.

- **schooner** a ship with two or more masts, as well as fore and aft sails.

- **profligate dissipation** extravagant spending.

- **John Greenleaf Whittier** (1807–1892) American abolitionist and poet. Douglass quotes from Whittier's poem "The Farewell: Of a Virginia Slave Mother to her Daughter Sold into Southern Bondage."

CHAPTER IX

Douglass returned to Master Thomas Auld's household in St. Michael's, Talbot County, Maryland, in March 1832. His new master gave him little food to sustain himself, for Auld was born poor and only acquired property and slaves through marriage. Douglass and other slaves were apparently very contemptuous of him. Douglass describes Thomas as "a slaveholder without the ability to hold slaves . . . [and] incapable of managing his slaves either by force, fear, or fraud." Thomas Auld became religious during Douglass' stay with him but his newfound Christianity did not make him any kinder. Instead, Thomas "found religious sanction for his cruelty" and quoted scriptures while whipping slaves. After nine months, Thomas found Douglass unmanageable and decided to "lend" him for one year to Edward Covey, a poor farmer who was known as a superb slave breaker. Slave owners who could not control their slaves sent them to Covey for "training"; in return, Covey had free use of these slaves for the farms that he rented.

Commentary

Even as a slave, Douglass recognized that there were class differences among slave owners. Those born poor and not used to owning slaves were the least competent in handling slaves. As a result, they could be exceedingly mean. Thomas Auld was obviously one such person. He apparently tried his best to appear noble and strong but manifested only a mean and cowardly spirit. Again, Douglass criticizes the vicious and loudly self-righteous Christianity of slave owners. The greatest hypocrites were those who quoted chapter and verse of their religion but were savagely cruel to their slaves.

- **religious sanction** Divine authorization.

- **He that knoweth . . . many stripes.** The passage is from Luke 12:47.

CHAPTER X

Douglas spent a year (1833) with Covey, during which he was frequently and brutally whipped. Having spent considerable time in the city, Douglass was not familiar with farm instruments and techniques. Because of this unfamiliarity, he made mistakes and was continually punished. Covey pushed his slaves to the limit, making them work long hours, and he constantly spied on them to make sure they did the work. Despite his professed religious piety, Covey saw profit in breeding slaves, so he bought a female slave and hired a married man to have sex with her for a year. Douglass confesses that witnessing this inhuman tyranny may have been the lowest point in his life for he contemplated killing Covey and ending his own life. Because Covey's farm was located on Chesapeake Bay, Douglass often saw ships from all around the world. The sight of their billowing white sails continually renewed his hope for an eventual escape.

One hot day in August, Douglass collapsed from fatigue, an event which led to matters that changed his life. Covey came by, kicked him, and gave him a beating. Although Douglass was bleeding profusely, he managed to escape and walked seven miles to St. Michael's, to ask Master Thomas for help. Although Thomas didn't believe Douglass' story and sent him back to Covey in the morning, he did allow him to stay for the night. On reaching Covey's farm, Douglass found himself the object of another beating. This time, however, Douglass ran into the cornfields and Covey couldn't find him.

Eventually, Douglass encountered Sandy Jenkins, a fellow slave who believed in the supernatural powers of certain plants. Sandy advised him to carry a certain root on his right side, an act which would make it impossible for any white man to harm him. Sandy believed that his own root had always saved him. To humor Sandy rather than argue with him, Douglass followed his instructions. To Douglass' surprise, when he returned to Covey's farm, Covey spoke kindly to him. A few days later, however, Covey pounced on him. This time, Douglass decided to physically resist. In the ensuing fight, Douglass gained the upper hand, and, after nearly two hours of wrestling and struggling, Covey finally gave up. Douglass recalls: "Covey at length let me go, puffing and blowing at a great rate, saying that if I had not resisted, he would not have whipped me half so much. The truth was, that he had not whipped me at all."

Douglass thinks that because Covey enjoyed a widespread reputation for being the region's best slave breaker, it provided him with plenty of free labor, and he didn't want to punish Douglass any further because doing so would be an admission of his having lost a physical fight. For the rest of Douglass' stay, Covey didn't touch him again. Douglass recalls: "This battle with Mr. Covey was the turning-point in my career as a slave. It rekindled the few expiring embers of freedom, and revived within me a sense of my own manhood. It recalled the departed self-confidence, and inspired me again with a determination to be free."

Douglass then discusses why slaveholders allowed slaves to celebrate holidays. If it were not for these days of rest, Douglass reasons, that there would be a multitude of slave insurrections. Holidays, he says, are opportunities for slave owners to encourage slaves to get drunk, and keeping slaves drunk is one way of keeping them servile.

Douglass' tenure with Covey ended after a year, and he was hired out to William Freeland in January 1834. Douglass calls Freeland "the best master I ever had, *till I became my own master.*" Freeland never hit Douglass but, more important, he didn't profess religiosity. Douglass tells the reader that religious slave owners are all unparalleled hypocrites, vicious and perverse.

Douglass soon grew attached to other slaves with whom he worked, and together they celebrated the Sabbath. Douglass became the Sabbath school instructor to his fellow slaves, a task he enjoyed greatly.

In 1835, Douglass began to think seriously about escaping. Together with several other slaves, he planned to steal a canoe and row up Chesapeake Bay. He even forged notes stating that they had permission from their owners to travel to Baltimore. This escape attempt failed, however, before it began because another slave betrayed them. The group was arrested and, to Douglass' surprise, Thomas Auld came to the jail and arranged for Douglass' release. Douglass, however, was considered the ringleader, so there was a general dislike of him in the community. Auld eventually sent him to live with his brother Hugh because he feared that someone might kill him. In turn, Hugh loaned Douglass to William Gardner, a ship builder.

For several months, Douglass was at "the beck and call of about seventy-five men," continually running errands for them. He might have stayed longer had it not been for a fight he had with his fellow white workers. The white carpenters were worried that free black men and slaves might become so proficient that they might eventually take their jobs away. One day, Douglass' fellow white apprentices started heckling and striking him. Because Douglass had promised himself after the Covey incident that he would fight back if physically mistreated, he struck back, and the ensuing fight nearly turned into a mob scene. Douglass was badly beaten and feared being lynched. In the end, however, he managed to escape.

Returning to Hugh Auld, he found his master and mistress surprisingly very kind to him. After taking care of his wounds, Auld took him down to Gardner to lodge a complaint. None of the white workers would testify on his behalf, though, and the words of black workers meant nothing.

Master Hugh didn't let him work with Gardner again; instead, he sent Douglass to work in the shipyard where he was foreman. Douglass took up the task of caulking (waterproofing boats) and soon became a skilled worker. In time, he started earning wages equal to the most skilled caulkers. All of his salary went to Hugh Auld, though, and this injustice made him more determined than ever to escape.

Commentary

This is the book's longest and perhaps most important chapter. Initially, Douglass returns to familiar themes, declaring again his contempt for histrionically religious slave owners. One such man was Covey, who bred slaves for profit. He was, however, one master who worked with his hands and thus knew what kind of work each slave could endure. His sneakiness and ability to deceive were his strengths to the degree that Douglass thinks Covey may have fooled himself into believing that he was a religious person.

Religion is an important element throughout Douglass' life and his *Narrative*. At the lowest points in his life, he speaks silently to God—for example, while watching the ships on Chesapeake Bay, sailing toward the Northern states. Some critics argue that it was at this point that Douglass became free, for once the mind is freed, the body will follow. Other critics, however, point to the fight that Douglass has with Covey as the real turning point, the moment when Douglass becomes psychologically free. Douglass himself believes that the Covey episode was significant.

Throughout his *Narrative*, Douglass repeatedly illustrates that Southern whites almost always close ranks when one of them is accused of a misdeed. We saw this behavior in Chapter IV, when the murder of blacks was condoned by the community. Similarly in this chapter, Thomas Auld won't listen to Douglass' complaints about Covey's barbarism.

The incident with Jenkins is puzzling. Douglass never lets us know whether he truly believed in the magical power of the root. Apparently, he was never "fairly whipped" again after the episode with Covey. Did Jenkins' root provide this protection? Douglass' opinion on this matter is unclear, for he says that he "was half inclined to think that the root [was] something more than I at first had taken it to be." Strangely, as a fervent Christian, his religion does not interfere with his adoption of this obviously pagan superstition. Whether this superstition harks back to an early African tradition is also unclear. It is possible that Douglass is making a sort of affirmation of his cultural roots when he follows Jenkins' instructions.

Douglass is fervent in his depiction of the reasons why slaveholders allow a certain number of holidays for their slaves. Keeping them working all the time would invite insurrections. Furthermore, holidays are occasions for slave owners to encourage drunkenness among the slaves. Douglass feels that slaves are so discouraged by their morning drunken stupors that they are "rather glad to go, from what our master had deceived us into a belief was freedom [that is, drunkenness], back to the arms of slavery." Douglass fails to mention another reason why owners provide holidays. Owners need holidays, too, for they can't spend all year managing and overseeing

Issac Bailey = Betsey

Charles Roberts = Pricilla   Henry   Harriet Bail

Eliza   Anna Murray (1st wife, d. 188

Charles   I

Captain Anthony = wife

Andrew   Richard   Lucretia = Thomas Auld =

John Sears = Amanda

=	married to
≠	has sex with

erick Douglass **Genealogy**

≠ Unknown male (possibly Captain Anthony)

≠ Ottilie Assing

= **Frederick** = Helen Pitts (2nd wife)

s   daughter (d. 1860)

owena Hamilton   Hugh = Sophia

Thomas

slaves. Implicit in Douglass' arguments is his criticism of his fellow slaves who allow themselves to be subjugated by alcohol.

Douglass' literacy provided him with a means of forging notes, stating that his group had their master's permission to travel. Douglass plays on the white man's **stereotyping** of the illiteracy of all blacks. But Douglass' first escape attempt failed because he was betrayed by a fellow slave; the slave system discourages solidarity among slaves. Unlike Southern whites who close ranks to protect their privilege, slaves are discouraged from establishing ties with each other. Douglass again makes an implicit criticism of his fellow slaves who do, or will not, unite for their gain. A united black population would definitely pose a threat to whites.

Later, Douglass again experienced the wrath of a united majority against the minority. After being beaten up in the shipyard and almost lynched, none of his fellow white workers would testify on his behalf that Douglass had been viciously mistreated. The white workers were also united against working with free blacks and slaves; they were afraid that black workers in the job market would eventually take jobs away from them. This fear is not unlike today's backlash against immigrants; many Americans today are indeed worried that immigrants will steal their livelihoods.

- **forte**   strength.

- **natural elasticity**   the ability to absorb tension; a resilience to harshness.

- **stern**   harsh.

- **rod**   five and a half yards.

- **quailed**   to be afraid; to show a loss of courage.

- **gratification**   enjoyment and satisfaction.

- **digressing**   rambling.

- **a severe cross indeed**   a heavy burden.

- **perdition**   hell.

- **calk** (or caulk)   to waterproof; to make watertight.

CHAPTER XI

Douglass escapes to the North in this chapter but is not forth-coming about how he managed this feat. He explains that his method of escape is still used by other slaves and thus he doesn't want to publicize it. Douglass adds that the **underground railroad** (an organized system of cooperation among abolitionists helping fugitive slaves escape to the North or Canada) should be called the "upperground railroad," and he honors "those good men and women for their noble daring, and applauds them for willingly subjecting themselves to bloody persecution," but he states emphatically that he is adamantly opposed to anyone revealing the means whereby slaves escape.

Douglass says that he needed money to escape, so he proposed to Hugh Auld that he "hire his time." In return for a set amount per week, Douglass gained the liberty of finding work; anything he made over the amount he promised to Auld was his to keep. "Rain or shine, work or no work, at the end of each week the money must be forthcoming, or I must give up my privilege." He relieved Hugh Auld from the responsibility of clothing, feeding, and finding work for him. For Douglass, this work situation meant suffering under sla-very, but also experiencing the anxiety of a free person (who must fend for him or herself in the job market). Nonetheless, he was determined to earn enough for his escape. Eventually he acquired enough money to get himself to New York on September 3, 1838.

The excitement of being free was soon tempered by loneliness and fear of being captured and kidnapped. In the North, there are plenty of "man-hunters," who are eager to take fugitive slaves back to their owners for a fee. Fortunately, he met David Ruggles, an abo-litionist who advised him to move to New Bedford, Massachusetts, about fifty miles south of Boston, where he could easily find work. Here, Douglass mentions for the first time his wife, Anna Murray (a freed woman whom he had met in Maryland), who joined him in New York City. They were married on September 15, 1838, and immediately traveled to New Bedford, where they stayed with Nathan Johnson, an abolitionist. Johnson suggested that Frederick change his last name in order to hide from slave hunters. Douglass explains: "I gave Mr. Johnson the privilege of choosing me a name, but told him he must not take from me the name of 'Frederick.' I must hold on to that, to preserve a sense of my identity." To replace

"Bailey," Johnson chose "Douglass," a character in Sir Walter Scott's long romantic poem *The Lady of the Lake*. Oddly, the name of the banished nobleman in that poem, James of Douglas, is spelled with a single *s*.

Douglass was greatly surprised at the wealth of luxuries in the North, for he had imagined that without slaves, Northerners must be living in poor conditions. Instead, he found the North to be refined and wealthy and without signs of extreme poverty. "The people looked more able, stronger, healthier, and happier than those of Maryland." Douglass was enterprising and soon found work loading a ship and managing various odd jobs. Unfortunately, he could not work as a caulker, for the white caulkers in New Bedford refused to work with a black person.

Another turning point occurred at this time. About four months after settling in New Bedford, Douglass chanced upon *The Liberator*, an abolitionist newspaper, and became more acquainted with the anti-slavery movement. While attending an anti-slavery convention on August 11, 1841, he spoke for the first time to an audience of white people at the urging of William Coffin, an abolitionist leader. Douglass ends his story by saying that as an ex-slave, he initially felt uneasy speaking to a white crowd, but he overcame feelings of inferiority and became an ardent orator and advocate of abolition.

Commentary

The newly-freed Douglass understood that his name was inseparable from his identity and chose to retain his first name. However, he deferred to his host in picking a new last name. *The Lady of the Lake* tells of a fugitive hero (James of Douglas) who redeems himself; it is a story which vaguely parallels Douglass' fugitive life.

In this final chapter, Douglass presents economic arguments against slavery. Foremost, slavery is a thief, he says, and the fruits of slave labor are enjoyed only by slaveholders. Douglass remembers that Hugh Auld was even disappointed that Douglass failed to bring as much as Hugh expected. Greed is clearly one of the fundamental ingredients of slavery—greed and power.

In New Bedford, Douglass learned that the **capitalist free market** could be perilous. A free market in which a person must fend for himself or herself is a difficult one, indeed, but Douglass certainly preferred that situation to a slave economy. Indeed, on reaching the North, Douglass was extremely happy to find work for himself, although he was unable to work in his chosen profession (caulking) because of racism. Douglass is much less critical and forthcoming about racism in the North (at least in this first version of his autobiography). There are several obvious explanations for this. First, he was still intoxicated with freedom in the North and any racism he experienced there would have been minor compared to what he underwent in the South. Second, he did not want to alienate his Northern hosts; as a fugitive, he certainly would not have wanted to confront racist Northerners who could inform slave hunters of his whereabouts. The power of slave hunters in the free states was a contentious issue for many years. Later, the Fugitive Slave Act of 1850 would legitimize fugitive slave hunting in free states.

Money became a necessary key for freedom, a key as important as knowledge, for Douglass needed money to buy his passage to New York (see Life and Background). He learned that a free market system indeed produces more wealth in the North. The white and black workers there were healthier, happier, and more prosperous than those in the South. Northern living conditions were better and the free market was simply a more efficient process. Machinery had replaced slave labor. Douglass heartily embraces the kind of capitalism he has seen in the North.

- **"I was hungry . . . he took me in."**   The passage is from Matthew 25:35.

- **habiliments**   clothing.

- **brethren**   brothers; fellow members.

APPENDIX

Certain editions of Douglass' *Narrative* conclude with an appendix. Douglass feels he may be misunderstood and wants to explain to the reader that he is not anti-religion. He makes it clear that he is only against the religion of slaveholders; for Douglass, their religion is far removed from the "Christianity of Christ." In fact, to embrace the latter as "good, pure, and holy, is of necessity to reject the other as bad, corrupt, and wicked." To be a Christian requires one to reject slavery.

Douglass ends by presenting a **parody** of a Southern church hymn called "Heavenly Union." In it, he pokes fun at Southerners who profess religion while "stinting negroes' backs and maws." He jibes at the preacher who gives his slaves only meager allowances of food and clothing, all the while urging them to "love not the world" (that is, indulge in worldly pleasures). And he exposes the "man-thief" (the slave trader) who lives very well from the profits of his trade. Finally, Douglass states that he hopes his little book will shed light on the institution of slavery and hasten its end. He pledges to fight for his "sacred cause" with the power of "truth, love, and justice."

Commentary

A religious context frames the entire *Narrative.* The abolitionists were, for the most part, religious people and many of their arguments were based on what *should* be the conduct of Christians. Abolitionists, Douglass included, wanted to distinguish their kind of Christianity from that of the slave owners. Abolitionism was clearly a part of their holy crusade.

Douglass ends his autobiography by reaffirming his name/identity ("I subscribe myself, Frederick Douglass"). Because slaves have no identity, by recognizing himself, Douglass is finally free.

- **votaries**   people devoted to a cause or religion.

- **Pharisees**   followers of an ancient Jewish sect, advocating strict observance of traditions and laws of the Hebrew faith. Jesus condemned them as hypocrites. Here, Douglass is comparing Christian slaveholders to Pharisees.

- **gnats**   insects or flies, especially those that are bloodsucking.

- **Pilate and Herod**   the Roman governor and ruler of Galilee, respectively, who condemned Christ to the Cross.

- **motes**   specks of dust.

- **Jack and Nell . . . Tony, Doll, and Sam**   names representative of slaves.

CRITICAL ESSAYS

"THE MEANING OF JULY FOURTH FOR THE NEGRO"

Frederick Douglass was a fiery orator and his speeches were often published in various abolitionist newspapers. Among his well-known speeches is "The Meaning of July Fourth for the Negro," presented in Rochester, New York, on July 5, 1852, a version of which he published as a booklet. It is often studied in literature classes today. Douglass moved to Rochester in 1847, when he became the publisher of *The North Star*, an abolitionist weekly. There were approximately 500 attendees who heard him speak, each paying twelve and a half cents.

He had been invited to speak about what the Fourth of July means for America's black population, and while the first part of his speech praises what the founding fathers did for this country, his speech soon develops into a condemnation of the attitude of American society toward slavery.

Douglass begins his speech by addressing "Mr. President, Friends and Fellow Citizens." Here, he is likely addressing the president of the Anti-Slavery Society—not the president of the United States. It is noteworthy that Douglass considers himself a citizen, an equal to the spectators in attendance. Throughout this speech, as well as his life, Douglass advocated equal justice and rights, as well as citizenship, for blacks. He begins his speech by modestly apologizing for being nervous in front of the crowd and recognizes that he has come a long way since his escape from slavery. He tells the audience that they have gathered to celebrate the Fourth of July, but he reminds them that the nation is young, and, like a young child, it is still impressionable and capable of positive change.

He touches on the history of the American Revolutionaries' fight for freedom against their legal bondage under British rule. He tells the audience that he supports the actions of these revolutionaries. Douglass thereby sets up an argument for the freeing of slaves. He reminds the audience that, in 1776, many people thought it was subversive and dangerous to revolt against British tyranny. In 1852, however, with hindsight, to say "that America was right, and England wrong is exceedingly easy." Similarly, he reasons, in 1852, people consider abolitionism a dangerous and subversive political stance. Douglass thus implies that future generations will probably consider his anti-slavery stance patriotic, just, and reasonable.

Douglass praises and respects the signers of the Declaration of Independence, people who put the interests of a country above their own. He concedes, however, that the main purpose of his speech is not to give praise and thanks to these men, for he says that the deeds of those patriots are well known. Instead, he urges his listeners to continue the work of those great revolutionaries who brought freedom and democracy to this land.

Douglass then asks a rhetorical question: "Are the great principles of political freedom and of natural justice, embodied in that Declaration of Independence, extended to us [blacks]?" He pushes forward his thesis: "This Fourth July [sic] is *yours*, not *mine*" [italics his]. Indeed, he says, to ask a black person to celebrate the white man's freedom from oppression and tyranny is "inhuman mockery and sacrilegious irony." By "sacrilegious," he means the evil defilement of sacred American ideals—democracy, freedom, and equal rights.

The real subject of his speech, he concedes, is American slavery. He condemns America for being untrue to its founding principles, its past, and its present. The audience must fulfill what the founders of the country advocated. To the slave, Douglass tells the audience, "your 4th of July is a sham; your boasted liberty, an unholy license [for enslaving blacks] . . . your shouts of liberty and equality, hollow mockery."

Douglass spends the next part of his speech pre-empting some of the arguments that theoretical opponents might make. As for the mildly sympathetic spectator who complains that the abolitionist fails to make a favorable impression by constantly denouncing slavery rather than making persuasive arguments, Douglass retorts by saying that there are no more arguments to be made. He says there is no person on earth who would be in favor of becoming a slave himself. How can it be, therefore, that some people are in favor of imposing a condition on others that they would not impose on themselves? As for those who maintain that slavery is part of a divine plan, Douglass argues that something which is inhuman cannot be considered divine. He considers such a pro-slavery posture to be blasphemy because it gives cruelty a place in God's nature.

Douglass condemns the profits made from the slave trade, and, once again, he compares the treatment of slaves to that of animals. He mentions that in Baltimore, slave traders transported slaves in chains to ships in the dead of night because anti-slavery activism had made the public aware of the cruelty of that trade. Douglass recalls that when he was a child, the cries of chained slaves passing his house on route to the docks in the middle of the night had a chilling, unsettling effect on him.

Next, Douglass condemns the American churches and ministers (excluding, of course, abolitionist religious movements such as Garrison's) for not speaking out against slavery. The contemporary American church, by remaining silent and acquiescing to the existence of slavery, he argues, is more of an infidel than Paine, Voltaire, or Bolingbroke (three eighteenth-century philosophers who spoke out against the churches of their time). Douglass argues that the church, is "superlatively guilty"—superlative, meaning even more guilty—because it is an institution which has the power to eradicate slavery by condemning it. The Fugitive Slave Law, Douglass reasons, is "tyrannical legislation" because it removes all due process and civil rights for the black person. "For black men, there is neither law nor justice, humanity nor religion." (Under this Act, even freed blacks could easily be accused of being fugitive slaves and taken to the South.) The Christian church which allows this law to remain in effect, Douglass says, is not really a Christian church at all.

Douglass returns to his theme of American democracy and freedom. He criticizes American ideology as inconsistent. For him, while it professes freedom, it does not give *all* people that right. And while it advocates democracy in Europe and elsewhere, it does not grant it to all of its own people. Similarly, he argues that while the American Declaration of Independence states that "all men are created equal," American society creates an under-class of men and women.

To his opponents who believe that the Constitution permits slavery, Douglass offers the writings of Spooner, Goodell, Sewall, and Smith—four abolitionists whose essays "clearly vindicate the Constitution from any design to support slavery." Douglass sides with those activists who believe that the founding fathers meant to eliminate slavery and that the Constitution reflects this.

Douglass concludes on an optimistic note. He believes that anti-slavery sentiments will eventually triumph over pro-slavery forces. Nations, particularly Western countries, in the mid-nineteenth century were generally against slavery. In fact, slavery was banned and in the British colonies in 1834 and in the French colonies in 1848; politicians in those countries could no longer claim to support the rights of man while allowing slavery. He argues that no longer can the cruelties of American slavery be hidden from the rest of the world. Trade and commerce have opened up borders, and political ideas know no boundaries. Douglass closes his essay with a poem by Garrison entitled "The Triumph of Freedom," stressing the inevitable arrival of freedom and the abolitionist's promise to fight slavery "whate'er the peril or the cost."

THE AUTOBIOGRAPHY AS GENRE, AS AUTHENTIC TEXT

In the eighteenth century, autobiography was one of the highest forms of literary art. Fiction was deemed unworthy, while narration of facts was aesthetically and philosophically pleasing. This prevailing convention overwhelmed fiction to such a degree that many novelists passed their works off as non-fiction, sometimes by creating prefaces written by supposedly real characters, who vouched for the authenticity of the story. Whether readers really believed in the truth of these stories is hard to say.

Although Douglass wrote in the nineteenth century, his *Narrative* belongs to this tradition of the autobiography as a superior genre. Autobiography is thus an ideal genre for arguing a political position.

Benjamin Franklin's *Autobiography* is one of the best examples of the autobiography genre. Douglass was a reader of Franklin's works and emulated some of Franklin's rhetoric and style. Like Franklin, Douglass' narrative also depicts, in part, the author's rise from poverty to become a major figure in American society. Like Franklin, Douglass also stresses perseverance, sacrifice, hard work and success—values of an emerging American culture. Douglass admired the accomplishments of the framers of the Constitution and, in particular, Franklin's achievements. Indeed, during his lifetime, Douglass was described as a black Benjamin Franklin.

Douglass' *Narrative*, particularly in the first few chapters, presents evidence in an objective and almost scientific manner. This wealth of verisimilitude adds an authentic feel to the work. Douglass may have been aware that other autobiographers sometimes added emotions and personal opinions into narratives. In particular, eighteenth- and nineteenth-century Romantic writers tended to extol the virtues of emotion in their works. One of the most famous of these autobiographies is Jean Jacques Rousseau's *Confessions*, a work marked by extensive use of emotional rhetoric. Douglass' work is consciously void of melodramatic discourse; he presents the atrocities of slavery without sensationalism or the Gothic horrors of nineteenth-century Romanticism.

Douglass entitles his autobiography *The Narrative of Frederick Douglass, an American Slave, Written by Himself* to stress *his* authorship of the work. There were other slave narratives in his time, some told by former slaves to white writers, and Douglass wanted to distinguish his work from other such narratives. The phrase "Written by Himself" persuasively makes the entire text seem more authentic. Douglass was aware that, on publishing his work, there would be racists who would charge that a self-educated fugitive slave could not possibly be capable of writing such an astute document. His statement of authorship is thus a pre-emptive rhetorical strategy to counter such racist critics.

SLAVERY AS A MYTHOLOGIZED INSTITUTION

One of Douglass' central goals is to debunk the mythology of slavery. Mythologies are institutionalized beliefs or ideologies, often accepted without question by the public. Southerners and some Northerners held certain beliefs about slavery which helped them rationalize its existence.

First, some believed that slavery was justifiable because it seemed to be supported by passages in the Bible (1 Timothy 6:1–2; 1 Peter 2:18; Ephesians 6:5–9; Colossians 3:22–24:1). They pointed to accepted dogma regarding the descendants of Ham (a name traditionally believed to mean "black") being destined for slavery (Genesis 9:18–27). If, however, Douglass asks, the dark skin of Ham is said to be a sign of this curse, then why are mulattos—some of whom have skin not significantly darker than whites—also destined by birth to be slaves? Douglass exposes the hypocritical nature of Southern Christianity by showing that slave owners simultaneously broke the laws of God in their treatment of slaves—while professing fervent Christianity.

Some slave owners, of course, believed slavery must exist, for without it, the American economy would suffer. Douglass refutes this myth. In the North he has observed many more examples of wealth than he saw in the South. Moreover, workers seem happier laboring for their own benefit. In addition, machines are more efficient and have replaced some slave labor. Finally, Phillips (in his introduction to the *Narrative*) points to the emancipation of slaves in the British colonies as being positive proof that the institution of slavery is unnecessary. The British economy did not collapse when slavery was abolished on West Indian plantations.

Another myth held by Southerners was that Africans were intellectually inferior and deserved, or even needed, the white man's care. It was, as British writer Rudyard Kipling describes, "the white man's burden" to colonize, civilize, and Christianize non-Europeans. Some whites believed that slavery was a means of protecting and bringing Africans into the civilized era. But, as Douglass points out, slavery provides no such benefits. The very text itself is a testimony against the belief of black intellectual inferiority. In the preface, Garrison argues that any person, regardless of race, would lose "all reasoning power" if kept under slavery.

Finally, many Southerners had a romantic image of the institution of slavery, believing it to be an integral part of gracious, genteel Southern living. This image of the Old South exists up to the present day—fortified by such cultural icons as *Gone with the Wind*. In fact, however, as Douglass points out, many slave owners were far from rich and grand—many lived in modest conditions and were crass and mean. The reality of the grand and gracious South was far from the mythical images of gentility and noblesse oblige of Southern living. This romantic image myth about the South includes a belief that the slaves were happy being slaves. Douglass rebukes this image; slaves never sing because they are happy—they sing because they are sad.

Douglass condemns both whites and blacks who buy into this fraudulent mythology. He is aware that even blacks can be fooled into accepting these myths about their position in Southern culture. Douglass is particularly incensed and sad about the vast disunity among slaves. He mentions slaves fighting among themselves to determine whose owner is kinder. While there is considerable natural fellowship among slaves, he says, the system promotes disloyalty among slaves. Owners encourage slaves to betray other slaves; a traitor double-crosses Douglass and prevents his first escape attempt. Some slaves cast their lot with slave owners and not with fellow slaves in the false belief that their prospects were better as slaves.

Slave owners encouraging slaves to buy into this false belief was one of the most insidious aspects of the mythology of slavery.

SLAVERY IN THE UNITED STATES

The first African to arrive in the New World is believed to have accompanied Christopher Columbus on one of his voyages to the Americas; African slaves began arriving shortly after 1492. There are records of slaves being in Haiti by 1501. The first blacks arrived in the British colonies almost 200 years before Douglass was born. In August 1619, twenty blacks arrived in Jamestown, Virginia, not as slaves but as indentured servants. These workers were freed after an indentured period of servitude, often seven years. Poor whites from Europe also came to the colonies as indentured servants. Their indentured service was regarded as payment for their voyage across the Atlantic. But while these whites chose to be indentured workers, the Africans were forcibly brought here. However, the number of Africans in the colonies was relatively small throughout the seventeenth century. Toward the end of that century, Africans were brought to North America as slaves in larger numbers. The establishment of large plantations in the South encouraged the import of African slaves who were deemed more cost effective than indentured servants, and more hardy and able to resist European diseases than Native Americans.

Although African slaves were sent mainly to the South, some ended up in the North, as well. Massachusetts, Rhode Island, and Connecticut were the leading Northern slave colonies. At the beginning of the American Revolution, there were an estimated 16,000 slaves in New England. In all the colonies, there were probably about a half-million slaves at that time.

The weather and soil conditions in the North prevented plantation-oriented agriculture. Northern slaves in the pre-Revolutionary era were employed as skilled and unskilled workers on farms and ships and in factories and shipyards. Agriculture was the predominant industry in the South, and slaves were deemed the cheapest, reliable labor for working the land. Two types of work plan were imposed on slaves: the Gang Plan and the Task System. In the former, large groups of slaves toiled in the fields under the supervision of an overseer. In the latter, slaves were given individual tasks to fulfill. Urban slaves tended to work under the Task System. In the

South, only favored slaves were excused from toiling in the fields. As you may recall, the slaves on Colonel Lloyd's plantation thought it was an honor to run errands and perform assigned tasks around the big plantation manor.

Because British law did not specify the status of slaves, the colonists created their own slave codes, and these codes varied from state to state. In general, they denied civil rights to slaves, and punishment meted out to slaves was often harsher than that given to whites for the same crime. In effect, there were two different legal codes—one for whites, another for blacks.

The end of the Revolutionary War saw the beginning of a large increase in the number of freed blacks. About 5,000 blacks who fought against the British during the war were emancipated by their masters. Following independence, many Northern states instituted universal emancipation within their states. As a result, the number of freed blacks grew rapidly, as did the restrictive codes placed on them. Freed blacks were immediately seen as an economic threat to Northern whites, and these written and/or unspoken codes were designed to keep blacks subservient. Douglass, for example, was a victim of Northern racism when he attempted—and failed—to find work as a caulker in New Bedford, even though he was well qualified and had his own tools.

Throughout the first half of the nineteenth century, the question of slavery remained a thorny political issue in the United States. Because the anti-slavery movement in the North was itself divided, a united front against Southern interests never materialized—until the outbreak of the Civil War. Anti-slavery activists belonged to different political camps. The Garrison camp reminded its followers of a higher moral law, that of God, and demanded immediate cessation of slavery on moral grounds. Another faction, the Liberty party, sought to change the status of slaves through reform, through working within the political system. The Free-Soil party, which evolved from the Liberty party, while retaining an anti-slavery platform, wanted to forbid slavery only in the new states and territories.

The Fugitive Slave Act was part of a last-ditch attempt to preserve the Union. Instead, it intensified the differences between the North and South. In 1854, Northern Whigs, anti-slavery Democrats, and Free-Soil party members assembled in Ripon, Wisconsin, to form a new political organization, the Republican party. The anti-slavery forces greeted the nomination and subsequent election of Abraham Lincoln to the presidency in 1860 as politically positive for their cause. The Southern states, however, reacted by moving toward secession. In February 1861, the Southern states chose Jefferson Davis as the Provisional President of the Confederate States. With the attack on Fort Sumter in South Carolina by Confederate troops on April 12, 1861, the Civil War began.

THE FUGITIVE SLAVE ACT

The issues of slavery and the rights of states to decide for themselves the slave question dominated domestic politics in the first half of the nineteenth century. The Fugitive Slave Act of 1850 essentially grew out of existing state and federal laws regarding the capture of escaped slaves. Colonial-era laws in various Southern states rewarded persons who captured fugitive slaves and punished those who sheltered or concealed them. The freeing of slaves in the North and the opening up of new territories in the West made fugitive slaves a national issue. Because not all Northern states and new territories had fugitive slave laws, runaway slaves often found haven there and thus enraged Southern slaveholders.

The first Fugitive Slave Act, passed by Congress in 1793, stipulated that slave owners or their agents could arrest and return escaped slaves from any territory or state, provided that proof be given to a magistrate that the apprehended blacks were indeed fugitives. Anyone hindering the arrest or providing haven to fugitive slaves was also liable for arrest.

In the first half of the nineteenth century, as opposition to slavery in the North grew, the Fugitive Slave Act began to lose its bite. Abolitionists and other sympathetic Northerners ignored the 1793 Act, and activists established a secret network of safe havens for fugitive slaves, stretching from the Deep South to Canada: the Underground Railroad.

Congress passed another Fugitive Slave Act in 1850, as a concession to Southern states, in an effort to preserve the Union, and because the 1793 Act was essentially ineffective. Increasingly, the North was clashing with the South regarding the issue of slavery in new states and territories acquired from Mexico after the U.S.-Mexican War (1846–48). Finally, the South threatened to secede.

Congress then created the Great Compromise of 1850 as a last chance to preserve the Union.

The 1850 Fugitive Slave Act was but one measure in this Compromise. Other measures mandated that California become a free state, that the territorial legislatures of New Mexico and Utah tackle the question of slavery within their borders, that no slave trade be allowed in the District of Columbia, and that, because Texas lost lands to the newly created New Mexico territory, the Federal government would assume some of the debts of the old Texas Republic.

The North also promised to vigorously enforce this new Fugitive Slave Act. Specifically, the Act stipulated that U.S. commissioners, in addition to courts, could issue warrants for runaway slaves and that only a claimant's deposition was necessary to prove ownership of a slave. As a result, even freed blacks were sometimes forced into slavery by unscrupulous whites. Commissioners were rewarded for each fugitive returned to slavery, and thus it was profitable to rule in favor of the claimant. In addition, penalties for harboring slaves were increased; there was now a $1,000 fine, six months jail time, and an imposition of civil damages payable to the claimant.

Essentially, however, the Great Compromise of 1850 satisfied almost nobody. Both sides felt betrayed by the Compromise. Tension between the North and the South continued to grow over the issues of slavery and states' rights. Some Northern states countered the Fugitive Slave Act by enacting state laws nullifying its effects. In the end, the Great Compromise preserved peace for only ten more years.

SLAVERY IN MARYLAND

Like other border states such as Delaware and Kentucky, Maryland was politically and socially tied to both the North and the South. Its urban areas were primarily Northern in character but the eastern part of the state, around the Tidewater region (see map) had an agrarian economy which was supported by slaves. The plantations in the Tidewater area produced many agricultural products including corn, wheat, and tobacco.

The land area that eventually became Maryland was known to European explorers in the sixteenth century, but it didn't interest colonists until the English settled there in the seventeenth century. In 1632, Charles I of England granted George Calvert, the first Lord of Baltimore, land between the 40th parallel line and Virginia. Calvert, who was Catholic, wanted to create a safe haven for Catholics who were persecuted in England. As in Virginia, African slaves accompanied the English settlers to Maryland. Maryland remained a proprietary colony until the American Revolution.

Baltimore grew rapidly in the eighteenth century and became an important port. During the 1760s, Pennsylvanians and Marylanders clashed over the issue of their border. To settle this dispute, Charles Mason and Jeremiah Dixon surveyed the land to determine the border. Their survey resulted in the Mason-Dixon line, which later became known as the line dividing the slave and free states.

Marylanders were strong supporters of American independence. In 1774, an independent convention was held in Annapolis and representatives from each state attended. After the Revolutionary War, the Continental Congress assembled again in Annapolis to ratify the Treaty of Paris (the treaty granting independence to the U.S.) and to accept George Washington's resignation from the Continental Army.

In the early nineteenth century, Maryland grew economically, as ships built in Maryland increasingly conducted international commerce, supplying European nations embroiled in the Napoleonic Wars with supplies. After the British were defeated in the War of 1812, Maryland expanded economically with railroads, public roads, and canals. Agriculture, however, continued to be an important element of the state's economy, with African slaves providing the labor on plantations.

There were, according to the U.S. Census of 1860 (the last census before the Civil War), 87,189 slaves, 83,942 free colored persons, and 515,918 whites in Maryland. When the Civil War began, troops from the North passed through Maryland to protect Washington, D.C., from Southern forces. However, on April 19, 1861, a mob from Baltimore attacked these troops, and Northern troops subsequently occupied Maryland during the remainder of the Civil War in order to ensure its allegiance to the Union. In fact, however, Marylanders fought on both sides of the War, and the battles of Monocacy, Sharpsburg (or Antietam) and South Mountain were fought in Maryland. In the post-Civil War years, Maryland grew rapidly and experienced significant urban and industrial expansion. As a result, the state became increasingly Northern in character.

DOUGLASS' CANONICAL STATUS
AND THE HEROIC TALE

Frederick Douglass was certainly not the only slave who wrote a narrative about his or her condition. Other slaves like Olaudah Equiano, Harriet Jacobs, and Phillis Wheatley also wrote important autobiographies. Douglass' slave narrative, however, remains the most popular and the most widely studied slave autobiography in high schools and colleges. What are the reasons for Douglass' canonical status? Perhaps the answer lies first in the fact that Douglass' life embodies the American spirit and ideology—that is, in Douglas's story, we have the heroic tradition of the underdog rising to become a success. In fact, as Americans, we are sometimes so entrenched in this dominant ideology that we forget it is not universally embraced around the world.

Second, because other slave narratives do not necessarily espouse and advocate notions which "fit" this American ideology, Douglass' *Narrative of the Life of an American Slave* succeeds in ways which others do not. Douglass is so appealing because although we may never fully understand his Otherness, his state of being unconditionally outside of the American mainstream of power and privilege, he creates a character who is understandable in our own dominant ideological terms. Most of us may never identify with his sufferings but we certainly can regard his spirit, values, and heroism as ours. This ideology includes a belief in the value of knowledge, empowerment, and enterprise, as well as the ability to create one's destiny.

For Douglass, knowledge meant—and led to—empowerment. We encounter his credo in the first paragraph of the *Narrative*. The need for information about himself was important enough to be "a source of unhappiness to [him] even during childhood." This concept of "knowing one's self" is one of the basic tenets of Western civilization. Ever since the ancient Greeks, the West has placed great value on self-discovery and self-knowledge.

For Douglass, not only self-knowledge, but knowledge itself was paramount—even knowledge of seemingly small talents—such as the ability to produce counterfeit documents. By learning how to read and write, Douglass had an opportunity to exploit the Southern stereotypical image of slaves. He was determined to reach his goal of being literate. In fact, during his early years, he developed diverse strategies to learn to read and write, including conning neighborhood children in Baltimore to teach him and copying letters he found at the shipyard and at home. His enterprising nature and dogged determination have a special place in American mythology and in its ideology. This ideology, championed by New England Transcendentalism (for example, Emerson's "Self-Reliance" and Thoreau's "Resistance to Civil Government"), is part and parcel of our nation's character. Our sympathy for Douglass is not mitigated even though he cons his childhood friends to teach him to read, because his goals—freedom, education, and self-reliance—are morally noble and thus his means are justified.

Douglass considered slavery to be an economic institution that was antithetical to learning. It reduced slaves to unthinking beasts, for as Master Auld explained: "Learning would spoil the best nigger in the world. It would forever unfit him to be a slave." Education was the path toward freedom, and, through his self-education, Douglass discovered the existence of abolitionist forces which sustained his hope of escaping to the North. This logocentric paradigm, coupled with the inability of antebellum Southern whites to consider that blacks could exist within this paradigm—that is, to be literate— offered Douglass unique openings. His ability to write enabled him to forge a pass for himself and other slaves in an escape attempt.

We admire his enterprising spirit. We applaud his attempts to negotiate, while a slave, for a "work-for-hire" status. By exchanging bread with neighborhood children for writing lessons, Douglass is, in essence, an entrepreneur. Arriving in New Bedford, he found his first job—unloading ships and working as a day laborer. Indeed, because his only commodity was his body, he made his sales pitch simply by approaching potential customers. Salesman, orator, entrepreneur, capitalist, Douglass thrived in these free market conditions. Capitalism demands absolute freedom in market transactions, but a slave economy, which does not always allow for the strongest or best to prevail, is inefficient.

Alongside his belief in the value of education, Douglass also believed in the individual's ability to create his own destiny. This tenet has been, of course, a dominant philosophy in the West since at least the European Enlightenment and one which New England Transcendentalism wholeheartedly embraced. (New England Transcendentalism, which still dominates American culture to this day, emphasizes hard work and personal success; an example of Transcendentalism today is the "Just Do It" slogan.) Douglass wrote at a time when the question of personal destiny was not unrelated to that of national destiny or the doctrine of Manifest Destiny. Personal, economic, and political gains would ultimately also benefit the nation. Consequently, our national ideology is also part of our personal belief. Until the end of his life, Douglass was a believer and a participant in the American Dream.

DOUGLASS' OTHER AUTOBIOGRAPHIES

Frederick Douglass wrote two more memoirs about his life: *My Bondage and My Freedom* (1855) and *Life and Times of Frederick Douglass* (1881). Both of these autobiographies are much longer than the *Narrative* and provide more of Douglass' views about racism and civil rights in the South, as well as in the North. However, the *Narrative* is more often taught in classes today than the other two books. Recent historical scholarship has focused attention on the minor discrepancies in the three versions. For example, in the last version (1881), Douglass denies having any knowledge of who his father was. Yet in the *Narrative* (1845), Douglass strongly implies that a white man, perhaps his master, was his father. Such inconsistencies have led scholars to argue that Douglass modified his autobiographies in order to suit changing politics. It is true that in the later part of his life, Douglass was more concerned with racial pride and seemed eager to suggest that his black heritage alone contributed to his success.

My Bondage and My Freedom is basically a continuation of the *Narrative*. In an early chapter, he gives more information about his mother, who "was the *only* one of all the slaves and colored people in Tuckahoe" who could read. Douglass admits that he doesn't know how a field hand could have gained this knowledge. Nevertheless, he thinks his thirst for knowledge came from his mother and not from his unknown white father. The underlying rationale for this assertion is to rebuke claims by racists who say that blacks are unintelligent and "uneducatable," or those who argue that Douglass must have inherited his intelligence from his white father. Douglass confirms that even the most abused field slave could learn to read; therefore, his capacity for intellect and love of learning could well have been inherited from his mother.

In *My Bondage and My Freedom*, Douglass reports gaining fame because of his abolitionist lectures and the publication of the *Narrative*. Accordingly, as his reputation grew, Douglass fled to England to prevent the possibility of arrest and a return to slavery. He tells the reader that onboard ship to England, he was not allowed to occupy a first class cabin because of his race. Nevertheless, because of his fame, many of the passengers came to see him in the steerage compartment, and they invited him to present his lectures to all the passengers of the ship. In this book, Douglass doesn't dwell much on the twenty-one months he spent in Great Britain, where he met many supporters of abolitionism. He does, however, voice his opinion about segregation on public transportation. Evidently, the British considered the American practice of segregation on public trains and ships outrageous. Editorials in *The London Times* and other papers condemned this practice, creating so much publicity that the Cunard line, which Douglass took to and from England, ended racial segregation on its steamships.

In the final chapter of *My Bondage and My Freedom*, Douglass tells stories about his endeavors to end segregation on trains in New England. On one occasion, he refused to give up his seat and move to the *"Jim Crow car"* (italics his). He fought physically with many conductors and passengers, disrupting many train schedules before the state of Massachusetts was finally compelled to forbid racial segregation on trains. Douglass ends his book by promising to use his voice and pen to "promote the moral, social, religious, and intellectual elevation of the free colored people . . . [and] advocate the great and primary work of the universal and unconditional emancipation of my entire race."

My Bondage and My Freedom was written when slavery was still in effect, and Douglass still refused to divulge his means of escaping from Baltimore to New York. He did not want to jeopardize those friends who helped him escape.

In *The Life and Times of Frederick Douglass* (1881), published sixteen years after the Civil War, when slavery was no longer a legal matter, Douglass reveals how he escaped. He borrowed identification papers from a friend, a free black sailor, and simply took the train to New York City.

My Bondage and My Freedom ends Douglass' story in 1855, when he was still a member of the Garrisonian wing of the abolitionist movement. In *Life and Times*, he describes how he became a close friend of John Brown, the leader of a movement dedicated to ending slavery through armed resistance and slave uprisings. Douglass then tells the reader that Brown originally planned to raid Harper's Ferry in 1858 but had to postpone the raid for a year when plans for the attack were leaked by a traitor. Douglass knew about the 1859 raid well in advance; in fact, he provided financial and spiritual support for Brown's venture, even though he never felt fit enough to be a part of a military operation. Brown was arrested while Douglass was lecturing in Philadelphia, and, learning about Brown's arrest, he telegraphed his own son Lewis in Rochester, New York, and asked him to secure and hide Brown's letters. Predictably, U.S. marshals soon arrived to question and search Douglass' household in Rochester. Douglass returned to Rochester and pretended that he was heading for Michigan. Instead, he left for Canada, and, on November 12, 1859, he left Quebec for England.

When the Civil War began, Douglass began working to recruit freed blacks into the Union army. He had an audience with President Lincoln and urged him to persuade President Davis of the Confederate States to forbid the South from executing black prisoners of war. He also asked Lincoln to mandate that black soldiers be paid the same wages as white soldiers. Lincoln didn't offer such guarantees. Instead, he told Douglass that black soldiers had more to gain from this war than whites and should therefore accept lower wages, at least for the time being. In his memoirs, Douglass expresses great admiration for Lincoln's compassion and humanity, but he disagrees with Lincoln on several points. For Douglass, Lincoln was more concerned about the preservation of the Union than he was with the issue of slavery. He suggests that Lincoln was even ready to allow slavery to continue—if the South would abandon the war and pledge loyalty to the Union. Following his meeting with the president, Douglass met with Secretary of War Stanton, who promised him a commission as assistant adjutant to the army's General Thomas. The army commission never arrived, and Douglass tells us that Stanton, after due consideration, probably changed his mind and felt that the Union was not ready for a high-ranking black officer. Interestingly, a small number of black soldiers were commissioned as officers during the Civil War, with a select few even reaching the rank of major.

Lincoln made public his intention to free all slaves in a speech on September 22, 1862. The Emancipation Proclamation took effect a few months later, on January 1, 1863. In *Life and Times*, Douglass says that this New Year's day will probably remain "a memorable day in the progress of American liberty and civilization." After the defeat of the South, Douglass lobbied hard to have Congress grant freed slaves citizenship. In the emotional period after Lincoln's death and the defeat of the South, Congress passed the Thirteenth Amendment (abolishing slavery), the Fourteenth Amendment (defining citizenship), and the Fifteenth Amendment (granting suffrage, voting rights, to blacks—a right denied American women until 1920).

After the Civil War, Douglass worked unceasingly to have women's rights recognized. In his memoirs, he expresses gratitude for the help the suffragettes gave to the abolitionist movement, and he reports that some people have characterized him as a "woman's-rights man," a title he is not ashamed of. It must be remembered that Douglass was very progressive for his era in believing in a woman's right to vote. Douglass proclaims in *Life and Times*, "Recognizing not sex, nor physical strength, but moral intelligence and the ability to discern right from wrong, good from evil, and the power to choose between them, as the true basis of Republican government, to which all are alike subject, and bound alike to obey, I was not long in reaching the conclusion that there was no foundation in reason or justice for woman's exclusion from the right of choice in the selection of the persons who should frame the laws, and thus shape the destiny of all the people, irrespective of sex." His use of the term "Republican government" here refers not to the party but to a non-monarchical, democratically elected government.

In the remainder of his memoirs, Douglass recounts some of the more interesting (and sometimes unexpected) episodes which occurred in the latter part of his life. For a time after the Civil War, Douglass earned a comfortable living by giving lectures. After one particular lecture, Douglass was given a note, stating that Mrs. Amanda Sears, the daughter of Thomas and Lucretia Auld and granddaughter of Captain Anthony, his former master, was in the audience. After speaking with Amanda's husband, John, Douglass was invited to visit their home. Although there were many women in that house, Douglass immediately recognized Amanda Auld, despite not having seen her for several decades. Afterward, Amanda and Douglass began a long-lasting friendship, developing mutual respect and admiration for each other.

Amanda's father, Thomas Auld, was still alive in 1877, and on his deathbed he requested to see Douglass. The reader may remember that in the *Narrative*, Douglass presents Auld as an uncaring, cruel, and hypocritical slaveholder. Douglass recalls: "But now that slavery was destroyed, and the slave and the master stood upon equal ground, I was not only willing to meet him, but was very glad to do so." The sight of the incapacitated and bedridden Auld brought tears to Douglass' eyes. It was an emotional meeting because both men were at first too choked with emotion to speak. Thomas Auld had read Douglass' *Narrative* and wanted to correct a point made in it about Douglass' grandmother. Auld assured Douglass that he had taken good care of Douglass' grandmother in her old age and that he certainly did not abandon her to die in her cabin. Douglass then told Auld that he had indeed incorrectly reported the incident in the *Narrative*, and he regarded both Auld and himself to be victims of a cruel system.

On this trip to St. Michael's, Maryland, Douglass also met the former sheriff who had locked him up when he attempted his first escape. Now, the former sheriff was among many who warmly welcomed his visit. Clearly, in *Life and Times*, Douglass wants to forgive the sins of a previous generation and move on to a new and brighter era of American civilization. He reports that the descendants of his former oppressors now treat him as an equal: "The abolition of slavery has not merely emancipated the negro, but liberated the whites." (**Note**: In the *Narrative*, Douglass spells *St. Michael's* with an apostrophe; today, the name of the town is spelled without an apostrophe.)

Douglass cautions, however, that prejudice continues to exist in American society. He describes his problems with public transportation on occasion because of his race.

Sadly, in the years preceding and following Douglass' death, the increasing use of segregation denied blacks the rights accorded by the Thirteenth and Fourteenth Amendments. A year after Douglass' death, the U.S. Supreme Court ruled that segregation was legal under the Constitution; the "separate but equal" doctrine was not fully overturned until the Civil Rights Act of 1964.

Douglass ends his *Life and Times* with a warning about the rise of Jim Crow laws and the imposition of near-slavery status on blacks in the South. The North "did not deprive the old master class of the power of life and death which was the soul of the relation of master and slave. They [whites] could not of course sell them [former slaves], but retained the power to starve them to death, and wherever this power is held, there is the power of slavery." In effect, Douglass says, economic slavery can be just as devastating as legal bondage. But Douglass remained a believer in enterprise and capitalism. For him, money and success lead to civil and political rights. Douglass' parting advice is compelling but simplistic; he urges blacks to save their money. "Every dollar you lay up, represents one day's independence, one day of rest and security in the future. If the time shall ever come when we shall possess in the colored people of the United States, a class of men noted for enterprise, industry, economy, and success, we shall no longer have any trouble in the matter of civil and political rights."

REVIEW QUESTIONS AND ESSAY TOPICS

(1). Why do you think it was important for slave owners to keep slaves ignorant about their birthdays and parentage? Douglass opens his story by telling us that he is troubled by not knowing when he was born. Why is this fact so important to him?

(2). List the turning points in Douglass' life. To what extent did his "take-charge" attitude create these turning points?

(3). Douglass presents much of his narrative in a factual tone and avoids personal opinions, yet the story is full of emotion. How is this possible? Where do you find evidence of emotion?

(4). What kind of hero is Douglass? Does his heroism come from his physical or mental state? Or does it come from both? Of the two types of heroes (physical or mental), which would he consider himself?

(5). In Chapter II, Douglass expresses his belief that education will set him free. What does he mean by this? Is this essentially an optimistic view? If he could visit us today, do you think he would still hold this view?

(6). Examine the films *Roots* and *Glory*, as well as music videos of Public Enemy; how do they portray slavery and black-white relationships in nineteenth-century America? Discuss the films and videos in terms of Douglass' *Narrative.*.

(7). Compare Douglass' depiction of the struggle of African Americans in white America with the narratives of such black writers as Maya Angelou, bell hooks, Alex Haley, Alice Walker, and Toni Morrison. In what ways can Douglass' influence be seen in the works of later black writers?

(8). Douglass' marriage to his white secretary in the later part of his life caused considerable discomfort among his white and black friends and acquaintances. Douglass had this to say about his marriage: "They would have no objections to my marrying a person much darker in complexion than myself, but to marry someone much lighter, and of the complexion of my father rather than my mother, was, in the popular eye, a shocking offense." To what extent have attitudes regarding interracial marriage changed? From his *Narrative*, what can you discern about his opinions regarding interracial marriage and/or procreation?

(9). The interracial concerns and problems Douglass expressed still affect us today. How will these problems diminish? Consider a disunited and disenfranchised African-American population, alcoholism/drug addiction among African-Americans, and the matter of whites fearing that minorities will take their jobs away.

(10). Various critics have placed Douglass' *Narrative* within the genres of Romanticism and also that of Realism. Does it belong to either category? Justify your claims.

(11). The underlying assumption and philosophy of Douglass' *Narrative* is that humans can (and must) create their destiny. Comment on Douglass' philosophy, citing examples and illustrations.

(12). Several times in his *Narrative*, Douglass expresses his view that slavery is bad for both white and black America. In what ways is slavery detrimental to the South?

SELECTED BIBLIOGRAPHY

SELECTED WRITINGS OF FREDERICK DOUGLASS

The best source of information about Frederick Douglass remains himself. Douglass wrote the following three autobiographies:

DOUGLASS, FREDERICK. *Narrative of the Life of Frederick Douglass, an American Slave, Written by Himself.* Boston: Anti-Slavery Office, 1845.

_____. *My Bondage and My Freedom.* New York: Miller, Orton, and Mulligan, 1855.

_____. *Life and Times of Frederick Douglass, Written by Himself.* Hartford, Connecticut: Park Publishing Co., 1881.

His collected speeches and articles can be found in:

BLASSINGAME, JOHN W. *The Frederick Douglass Papers.* New Haven: Yale University Press, 1979.

Some of his more famous speeches and articles are listed below. (Unless otherwise indicated, they appear in Blassingame's collection.)

"The American Apocalypse," Rochester, New York, June 16, 1861.
"Capital Punishment Is a Mockery of Justice," Rochester, New York, October 7, 1858.
"Fighting the Rebels with One Hand," Philadelphia, January 14, 1862.
"John Brown and the Slaveholders' Insurrection," Scotland, January 30, 1860.
"Letter to His Old Master," appears in *My Bondage and My Freedom.*
"The Meaning of July Fourth for the Negro," Rochester, New York, July 5, 1852.
"The Proclamation and a Negro Army," New York, February 6, 1863.

"The Slaveholders' Rebellion," New York, July 4, 1862.

"Slavery and the Irrepressible Conflict," Geneva, New York, August 1, 1860.

"Slavery and the Limits of Nonintervention," England, December 7, 1859.

SOURCES FOR BACKGROUND INFORMATION

BOWMAN, JOHN S. (ed.) *Civil War Almanac*. New York: Bisson Books, 1982.

CHASE, HAROLD W. *Dictionary of American History*. New York: Charles Scribner & Sons, 1976.

HORNSBY, ALTON, JR. *Chronology of African-American History, Significant Events and People from 1619 to the Present*. Detroit: Gale Research, 1991.

ROLLER, DAVID, et al. (eds). *Encyclopedia of Southern History*. Baton Rouge: Louisiana State University Press, 1979.

CRITICAL WORKS

BLIGHT, DAVID W. "The Private Worlds of Frederick Douglass," *Transition: An International Review*, 1993, 61, 161–68.

CARSON, SHARON. "Shaking the Foundation: Liberation Theology in Narrative of the Life of Frederick Douglass," *Religion and Literature*. Notre Dame, Indiana: University Press. 1992 Summer, 24:2, 19–34.

GATES, HENRY LOUIS, JR. "A Dangerous Literacy: The Legacy of Frederick Douglass." *The New York Times Book Review*, May 28, 1995. 3.

_____. "From Wheatley to Douglass: The Politics of Displacement," *Frederick Douglass: New Literary and Historical Essays*. Cambridge: Cambridge University Press, 1991.

GIBSON, DONALD B. "Christianity and Individualism: (Re) Creation and Reality in Frederick Douglass's Representation of Self," *African-American-Review*, Terre Haute, Indiana, 1992 Winter, 26:4, 591–603.

JAY, GREGORY S. "American Literature and the New Historicism: The Example of Frederick Douglass," *Boundary 2: An International Journal of Literature and Culture*. Durham, North Carolina, 1990 Spring, 17:1, 211–242.

MAILLOUX, STEVEN. "Misreading as a Historical Act: Cultural Rhetoric, Bible Politics, and Fuller's 1845 Review of Douglass's Narrative," *Readers in History: Nineteenth-Century American Literature and the Contexts of Response.* Baltimore: Johns Hopkins University Press, 1993.

TUTTLETON, JAMES W. "The Many Lives of Frederick Douglass," *The New Criterion*, New York, 1994 February, 12:6, 16–26.

YARBOROUGH, RICHARD. "Race, Violence, and Manhood: The Masculine Ideal in Frederick Douglass's 'The Heroic Slave,'" *Frederick Douglass: New Literary and Historical Essays.* Cambridge: Cambridge University Press, 1991.

ZAFAR, RAFIA. "Franklinian Douglass: The Afro-American as Representative Man," *Frederick Douglass: New Literary and Historical Essays.*Cambridge: Cambridge University Press, 1991.

ZEITZ, LISA MARGARET. "Biblical Allusion and Imagery in Frederick Douglass' Narrative," *College Language Association Journal.* Atlanta, Georgia, 1981 September, 25:1, 56–64.

Think Quick

Now there are more Cliffs Quick Review® titles, providing help with more introductory level courses. Use Quick Reviews to increase your understanding of fundamental principles in a given subject, as well as to prepare for quizzes, midterms and finals.

Do better in the classroom, and on papers and tests with Cliffs Quick Reviews.

Your Guides to Successful Test Preparation.

Cliffs Test Preparation Guides

• *Complete* • *Concise* • *Functional* • *In-depth*

Efficient preparation means better test scores. Go with the experts and use *Cliffs Test Preparation Guides*. They focus on helping you know what to expect from each test, and their test-taking techniques have been proven in classroom programs nationwide. Recommended for individual use or as a part of a formal test preparation program.

Advanced Placement Demands Advanced Preparation

Cliffs Advanced Placement® study guides are designed to give students that extra edge in doing their best on these important exams. The guides are complete, concise and focused providing you with all the information you need to do your best. Study with Cliffs Advanced Placement study guides for the kind of score that will earn you college credit or advanced standing.

- Thoroughly researched strategies, techniques and information
- Analysis of multiple-choice and essay questions
- Written by testing experts

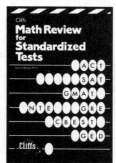

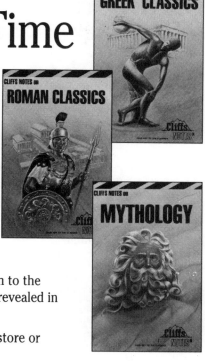